Dead in the Water

Robin Stevenson

Orca sports

D1020391

Orca Book Publishers

Library and Archives Canada Cataloguing in Publication

Stevenson, Robin H. (Robin Hjørdis), 1968-
Dead in the water / written by Robin Stevenson.

(Orca sports)
ISBN 978-1-55143-962-4

I. Title. II. Series.

PS8637.T487D42 2008   jC813'.6   C2007-906807-3

Summary: Simon gets a crash course in foul weather sailing,
teamwork and environmental protection.

First published in the United States, 2008
Library of Congress Control Number: 2007940554

Orca Book Publishers gratefully acknowledges the support for its publishing
programs provided by the following agencies: the Government of Canada
through the Book Publishing Industry Development Program and the Canada
Council for the Arts, and the Province of British Columbia through the BC Arts
Council and the Book Publishing Tax Credit.

Cover design by Teresa Bubela
Cover photography by Getty Images
Author photo by David Lowes

Orca Book Publishers
PO Box 5626, Stn. B
Victoria, BC Canada
V8R 6S4

Orca Book Publishers
PO Box 468
Custer, WA USA
98240-0468

www.orcabook.com
Printed and bound in Canada.

11 10 09 08 • 4 3 2 1

To Cheryl

Acknowledgments

Thanks to Ilse Stevenson, for suggesting that I write about abalone poaching; to Bryan Jubinville of the Department of Fisheries and Oceans, for sharing his experience and expertise on the subject; and to Barb Peck and Bjarne Hansen, sailors extraordinaire, for all their input.

chapter one

The sky and the sea were almost the same shade of gray, and I wasn't sure which was wetter. Spray from the waves flew into the cockpit, cold and salty, and rain pelted down viciously from above. I shivered and gripped the wheel more tightly. Across the cockpit, the others were a blur of brightly colored Gore-Tex. I couldn't see a thing through my glasses.

The bow of the boat lifted on a huge wave and plunged down, landing with a shuddering crash. It felt like hitting cement. At least cement would be dry, I thought, as a sheet of icy water slapped the side of my head. My shoulders ached from hanging on to the wheel as ten tons of speeding fiberglass fought against me, trying to turn into the wind. We were heeled way over to one side, the starboard rail almost buried in the water. The sails needed to be adjusted, but no one was volunteering. I gritted my teeth and tried to ignore the queasiness in my stomach. If I threw up now, the others would never let me live it down.

Then Patrick yelled, "Man overboard!"

My heart leapt into my throat, and my stomach felt like I'd swallowed a chunk of ice. Who was it? I squinted through my rain-splattered lenses. The blur of Gore-Tex turned into Olivia and Blair. Joey was missing.

We all sprang into motion. Olivia grabbed the man-overboard pole and threw it into the water. Its weighted bottom and float would hold it upright, and the bright orange flag flying six feet above the water would be a lot easier to spot than a person's head.

I swallowed nervously. Joey's head. Olivia stood behind me at the stern, holding onto the rigging for balance and pointing at the flag. I couldn't see Joey. I couldn't see anything at all in the water. Just steep gray waves and blowing spray.

"Don't take your eyes off that flag and don't stop pointing," Patrick shouted to Olivia. His voice was almost drowned out by the wind. I tried frantically to remember the man-overboard procedure. I'm not stupid, but my brain sort of freezes up under pressure.

"Get the boat on a beam reach," Olivia hissed into my ear.

"Olivia! Do your own job and let Simon do his." Patrick sounded annoyed, but I could have kissed her. Not that she'd be likely to let me.

Beam reach. I quickly twisted the wheel around, and the boat turned slowly to the right. Now the wind was coming at us sideways, or to use the correct sailing term, over our port beam. Instantly the boat flattened out to a more reasonable angle, the noise of the wind subsided to a muffled howl, and my brain started working better.

I glanced over my shoulder. Behind us, the flag was barely visible, its urgent orange hidden in the troughs between the waves. I hoped Joey hadn't been knocked out when he fell overboard. I hoped he'd swum to that pole and was just waiting for us to come back for him. My instincts were screaming at me to turn around and head back toward the flag before we lost sight of it, but I knew I couldn't do it. If I tried to head back now, we'd pass right by Joey without getting close enough to help him. *Jeopardy*'s turning circle under sail was huge. I needed to give us some sea room to maneuver.

Blair and Patrick were on either side of me, ready to adjust the sheets—the ropes that control the sails—as soon as I gave the order. Now all I had to do was bring *Jeopardy* close enough to that orange flag. I wished someone else—anyone else—was at the helm for this. What if I messed up? What if Joey drowned? I had no idea if I'd gone far enough. I glanced behind me again. I couldn't see the flag at all now, just an endless jagged seascape of heaving gray water. I gripped the wheel harder, twisted it to port and took a deep breath. "Coming about!"

As *Jeopardy*'s bow swung slowly through the wind, the jib sail started to flap slightly. Quickly, Blair released the jib sheets and let the wind push the sail across to the other side. Patrick braced himself against the boat's motion, wrapped the port-side sheets around the winch and began cranking it in as fast as he could, his broad shoulders moving back and forth with the effort. We were now on a starboard tack and heading back toward that orange flag.

Now the big rescue was up to me, Simon Drake, five foot six and 120 pounds soaking wet. Which I was.

And I couldn't see the flag. Couldn't see a darn thing. I looked at Olivia for help. She shrugged, but she was still pointing, so I just kept heading in the direction where she'd last been able to see the flag. Patrick was right, I thought. Without a man-overboard pole, you'd never find a lost crew member. Not a chance. I imagined myself struggling in that cold water, mouth and eyes burning with salt, fighting for breath and seeing the boat sailing away, leaving me behind. I shuddered. Goose walking over your grave, my grandmother would have said.

I hoped not.

Suddenly the man-overboard pole appeared, riding a wave and flashing its orange flag against the rolling gray. My heart sped up. Blair sprinted up to the bow, ready for the rescue. We were flying along, the sails taut.

Closer, closer. I caught my breath. Too close. We were headed straight for the flag and unless...

"Heads up!" Patrick yelled. "Turn into the wind and ease the sheets to slow down!"

Too late. *Jeopardy* plowed straight into the orange flag and it disappeared under the water. I couldn't believe it. I was shaking so bad I could hardly grip the wheel. I hadn't seen Joey, but if he was holding that flag... I thought I might be sick.

"Nice one!" Blair yelled, a look of disgust on his face.

Patrick shook his head in mock sorrow. "Lucky it was a drill. If that had been a real person in the water, you'd just have killed him."

"Or her," Olivia put in. She sounded irritated, as usual.

I stared at them. Nothing was making sense. "Real person? But what about Joey?"

Then Joey's head popped up in the companionway hatch, a big grin on his face. "Did I miss something? I was just taking a dump. Man, that toilet stinks."

"Simon thought you'd gone overboard," Blair shouted. Everyone started to laugh. Even Olivia, who I didn't think knew how.

The boat gave a sickening lurch. I leaned over the rail to puke and tried to remember exactly what had made me think this sailing course would be a good idea.

chapter two

My family wasn't the kind that owned boats or even the kind that knew people who did. Mom and Dad worked hard, but their money went toward paying the rent, buying the groceries and picking up a weekly lottery ticket. Unless one of those tickets turned out to be a winner, we wouldn't be joining the yacht club anytime soon.

Not that my parents would want to, Dad especially. He thinks all sailors are rich snobs. Whatever. He has no idea what it's really like and no interest in finding out. It just annoys him that I want to sail instead of play football like he did. Personally, I think the sea is easily as tough an opponent as a whole football team.

Anyway, sailing is more than a sport. It's a way of life. For a guy with no connections, I've managed to log a fair number of hours under sail on racing boats. You start out as ballast—just extra weight where it's needed to help the boat go faster. You get yelled at a lot but you learn fast.

Racing's not what I want to do though. I want to be a delivery skipper. I want to sail those rich folks' boats across the oceans for them, deliver them to the Caribbean or the Mediterranean. They can have their lazy holidays in the sun. Me, I want to be out at sea.

At least I thought I did before this trip.

It had started out okay. We had all met up at the marina in Port Hardy, four teenagers who had all come here for a sailing course. Blair and Joey, brothers from Vancouver, were tall, well built and dressed in expensive Helly

Hansen rain gear. They were the junior version of the rich yachties my dad complains about. Olivia was all spooky black hair and major attitude. Patrick, our sailing instructor, greeted us with a crooked grin; then he took us down to the boat for a quick tour. It was a thirty-six-footer, a lot bigger than the racing boats I was used to.

"Choose a berth and leave your stuff there for now," Patrick told us. "If you need the head, it's on the port side, just aft of the V-berth. And here's the galley." He pointed at a sink and stove top.

"Uhh…" Joey looked lost.

"Head equals toilet. Berth equals bed. Galley equals kitchen," Olivia said, not even cracking a smile.

I snagged a narrow single berth tucked away at the stern and tossed my bag on it to stake my claim.

Olivia bent close. "You picked the coffin," she whispered.

"What do you mean?"

She nodded at the bed. "Just what it's called. 'Cause of the shape, I guess. You can't sit up in it." She narrowed her eyes at me. "Hope you aren't claustrophobic."

I met her eyes. Lime Slurpee green and just as icy. "Nope. Not me."

She shrugged. "I am." She glanced around the boat, and I followed her gaze. Joey and Blair were arguing over who would get which berth.

"I'll arm-wrestle you for this one," Joey said.

Blair started rolling up his sleeves.

"You two can share the V-berth," Patrick told them. He was leaning back against the stove, listening and watching with a half smile on his tanned face. I wondered what he was thinking and whether he was dreading being stuck on the boat with us.

"This boat is going to drive me nuts," Olivia informed me.

Cry me a river, I thought. I'd worked two crap jobs—at a gas station and a diner—and saved my ass off to get here, so she was looking for sympathy from the wrong guy. "Why did you come then?"

"My dad made me."

I rolled my eyes. I couldn't help it.

She didn't miss a thing. "What's your problem?"

"What's yours?"

Olivia stalked off, skinny shoulder blades practically twitching with irritation as she climbed the companionway steps.

Patrick chuckled. "Let's all go get some dinner. We have an early start tomorrow."

We trudged along in the cold drizzle, following Patrick down the docks. I was relieved when he stopped at a small restaurant near the harbor. I was starving.

My heart sank when we stepped inside. White tablecloths, candles, glossy hardwood floors. I didn't even have to look at a menu to know that I wouldn't be able to afford much more than a Coke.

I guess Patrick caught my expression, because he jumped in pretty fast. "Dinner's included. Halibut burgers and fries." He winked at me. "This is my family's restaurant."

"Sounds great," I said, surprised.

Olivia was looking at the menu. "Abalone? Abalone? Please tell me it's not..."

I stared at her. "What's the big deal?"

"Baloney? You want baloney?" Joey asked, bewildered.

Patrick cut in. "Relax, honey. It's imported."

She ignored me and Joey and kept talking to Patrick. "Would you mind not calling me honey? My name's Olivia."

Man, she needed to chill out. I nudged her. "You allergic to shellfish or something?"

She looked at me scornfully. "For your information, abalone in BC is a threatened species."

"Lots of places serve it," I argued. "The Chinese place we go to back home does."

"Yeah? Well, you should ask where it's from. Make sure it's not local."

I doubted anything they served was even fresh, let alone local. Anyway, now that I thought about it, it might have been mussels or clams or something. I shrugged. "So don't eat it."

"Don't worry," Olivia said. "I wouldn't."

The halibut burgers arrived at our table—big, juicy, dripping tartar sauce and

13

surrounded by huge piles of steaming hot fries. I licked my lips. Joey and Blair dug in.

"I'm a vegetarian," Olivia announced. "Are the French fries cooked in animal fats?"

I sighed. It was going to be a long week.

chapter three

The next day, we got up early and sailed out of the harbor. It was awesome: a gentle breeze was blowing, the water was calm, and we hummed along under full sail. A curious seal popped its head out of the water and watched us go by. Fishing boats motored past. I couldn't stop grinning. Patrick told us we were headed for Bull Harbour, up on Hope Island, and that we'd spend the night there. Tomorrow, he said, we'd round Cape Scott and start working our way south toward our eventual destination of Tofino. Wind and weather permitting, he'd added with a wink. That's why the course was eight to ten days—with sailing, you can't predict exactly how long a journey will take.

We had all signed up for an intermediate cruising course through the yachting association. We had to learn a whole list of practical skills as well as a book full of theory—everything from adjusting the sails to anchoring the boat to tying an unbelievable variety of knots. If I passed, I'd be qualified to bareboat charter—which basically means I'd be allowed to rent a boat from a charter company anywhere in the world. Of course, I couldn't afford to do that. Still, the official sailing qualification would help me to convince someone to take me on as crew. I'd be one step closer to my goal of becoming a delivery skipper.

We practiced man-overboard drills that morning—Patrick kept calling them that, despite Olivia's insistence that the correct term was "crew overboard." We practiced a ton of other stuff too—tacking and jibing to turn the boat, reefing sails to keep control in heavy weather and adjusting sails for maximum speed and comfort. The wind picked up around lunchtime, and the water got rough, kicking up a steep chop. *Jeopardy* started to pound into the waves, and suddenly lunch lost its appeal.

That was when Patrick yelled, "Man overboard!" and I made a total ass of myself. Joey couldn't stop laughing, and Blair kept punching my shoulder for some reason.

"You really didn't realize it was a drill?" Patrick finally asked, wiping the tears from his cheeks.

I shrugged sheepishly. "You sounded real serious, and then I couldn't see Joey..."

"Man." He shook his head.

"Spacey Drake," Joey said, cracking himself up.

After that, everyone started calling me Spacey instead of Simon. Everyone except Olivia, that is. I'd say she was being nice but I think she just wanted to do the opposite of what everyone else did. She was like that.

We made it up the channel between the islands and into Bull Harbour late that afternoon. I was glad when we got out of the waves and into the protected water of the anchorage. Sailors don't talk much about it, but seasickness is utter hell. Your mouth gets all gross feeling, like you have too much saliva. You yawn until your jaw aches, and you feel irritable and tired and achy and nauseated. And then you throw up, and you think that might help, but it doesn't help at all. It just goes on and on and on.

I didn't want to let on how lousy I was feeling, though obviously everyone noticed that I kept leaning over the edge and chucking up. Still, when we got into Bull Harbour I was the one up on the foredeck, lowering the heavy Bruce anchor into the calm dark water.

It was beautiful there. The water was so still it was shiny, and the trees along the shoreline were reflected as long dark fingers reaching out across the bay. The sky was a pearly gray, and once our engine was switched off, it was incredibly quiet. There was only one other boat there—a cabin cruiser, maybe a forty-footer, anchored a little closer to shore—and not a person in sight.

I wrapped the anchor rope around the cleat in a figure-eight pattern, twisting the last loop once to secure it.

Olivia appeared beside me. The girl had cat feet: even in the silence of this anchorage, I hadn't heard her coming. She nodded toward the cabin cruiser. "Odd, don't you think?"

"What's odd?"

"They have scuba gear on the deck."

I stared at her. "So they like diving. Lots of people like diving."

"I guess," Olivia said.

Patrick appeared on the deck and beckoned to us. We headed back to the cockpit and sat there, rubbing our sore muscles and waiting to hear what he had to say.

"For a first day," he drawled, "that wasn't too bad. You all have areas you need to work on though." He lit up a cigarette.

Olivia frowned. "Are you supposed to smoke while you're teaching?"

"My boat, honey. I make the rules." He winked. "Olivia, you're quick on your feet and you have an instinctive understanding of the how the wind works in the sails. What you need to work on is your attitude. Try acting like you want to be here, okay?"

She shrugged. "I didn't know we were being graded on our acting ability."

He shook his head in mock disgust and moved on. "Blair and Joey, you're big strong guys, but you need to understand the theory so you know what to do with all that muscle power. There's no point in cranking the sail in as tight as you can if we're sailing on a broad reach. If the wind is behind us, you need to let the sails out. You need to work with the wind."

Patrick took a drag on his cigarette and turned to me. "Simon, you're getting called Spacey for a reason. You've got the best understanding of sailing of anyone here, but most of the time you're off in your own world. You need to work with the crew. If the sails need adjusting, ask someone to do it instead of fighting the boat. We could've been going a good two knots faster if the sails had been trimmed properly."

"I was at the helm," I protested. "Trimming the sails wasn't my job."

He met my eyes. "But you were the only one who knew it needed to be done. I bet you've got some sore muscles now, right?" He glanced around at the others. "Did any of you notice the problem?"

They all shook their heads.

"Looked fine to me," Joey offered.

Patrick nodded. "That's what I thought. So, Simon? Try to be a bit more of a team player."

I stared at my runners and said nothing. Delivery skippers sail alone.

chapter four

We had a schedule worked out for cooking meals, and Olivia and I were on for dinner. Cooking isn't my thing, so I was a bit apprehensive. Fortunately it was very straightforward: *Jeopardy* had a surprisingly large freezer, and all we had to do was pull out a lasagna and stick it in the oven. Even I could manage that.

"I can't eat it," Olivia announced. "It's beef."

I picked up the package and pointed to the picture on the front. "Look at that. It doesn't look like beef. It's just a miscellaneous meat-like product. I bet it didn't come from a cow."

She just looked at me. "I'll make a salad."

"You're gonna get pretty hungry," I said. "There's steak kebabs on the menu for tomorrow night."

Olivia ignored me. She sat at the table and sliced up tomatoes and cucumber while I washed lettuce for a salad. She was fast: the knife flew up and down and the vegetables collapsed into neatly sliced and diced piles.

I tossed the greens into a large plastic bowl. "You worked in a restaurant or something?"

"Nope. I just concentrate on what I'm doing."

I could feel myself flushing. "What's that supposed to mean?"

"Nothing." She bit her lip.

I slammed the salad bowl down on the table harder than was strictly necessary. To be honest, I was a bit worried about this whole concentration thing. I'd been getting in trouble for zoning out my whole life. A couple of years ago, my teacher told my folks I should be on medication for it. Dad told them what they could do with their pills and that was the end of that.

"So, how come you're in such a bad mood?" I asked. I wasn't that interested, but I didn't want to think about the spacing-out thing anymore.

Olivia scooped the chopped veggies up and dumped them on top of the lettuce. "Told you already. I don't want to be here."

"So how come your dad made you?"

She wrinkled her nose. "He sails. He spends most winters down in the Caribbean on his boat and he wants me to come."

I couldn't keep the disbelief out of my voice. "He's in the Caribbean. On a boat. And you don't want to go?"

"His new wife is there too," Olivia said darkly. "His new wife who's about twenty-five and used to be his student."

"His student?"

"PhD student. Dad's a marine biologist."

I shook my head. "Whatever. I can't believe you're passing up a chance like that... Hey. Think your dad would take me instead?"

"I think he wants to bond with his daughter. So, no, probably not."

"Figures."

Olivia grinned at me. "Cheer up. And take the lasagna out before it burns to a crisp. I'm not eating it, but I'd hate for the cow to have died for nothing."

Over dinner—slightly blackened but none-theless delicious—Patrick quizzed us on the parts of the boat. I knew them all, and I took some small satisfaction in discovering that Blair and Joey did not. They might look like junior yacht clubbers, but they barely knew port from starboard, let alone the leech from the luff.

Blair and Joey were on dish duty, so Olivia persuaded me to go ashore with her in the dinghy. Not that she was particularly enjoying my company: She'd rather have gone alone, but Patrick had vetoed that idea. I didn't mind. I wanted to stretch my legs anyway.

The dinghy was a rubber Zodiac inflatable. They're fast enough with an outboard engine, but they're crap to row. It was a long way to shore, so I automatically started to lower the propeller into the water.

Olivia grabbed my arm. "No, don't spoil the quiet."

I rolled my eyes, but actually I didn't mind. It was really peaceful. All around us, the trees and the clouds were reflected in the water like it was a big dark mirror. I dipped the oars in and started to row.

"If I was a guy, you wouldn't have assumed you had to row," Olivia said.

I thought about that for a moment. "You can row back," I told her.

She grinned. "I was just teasing you." Then she frowned. "Hey, Simon...row past that other boat, okay?"

"Why?"

"Why not? We can say hello. They're our neighbors for tonight. We might as well be polite."

I narrowed my eyes at her. "Uh-huh." I didn't think politeness was usually high on her list of priorities. Nosiness, maybe, but not politeness.

"Come on. Why not?"

The cabin cruiser was a few hundred feet away, between us and the shore. I shrugged. "Sure. It's on the way."

We rowed in silence for a while, listening to the dip-splash of the plastic oars in the water. At one point a seal poked its head up right beside our dinghy, and we drifted for a while, watching while it stared at us. Neither of us said anything, but our eyes met and we both grinned. Some people would have had to talk about it, but Olivia wasn't like that. It was all right, hanging out with someone who didn't feel the need to talk all the time.

I glanced over my shoulder. We were getting close to the boat. I could see its name— *Salty Mist*—written in script on the stern. I lifted the oars out of the water and let our momentum carry us until we bumped alongside. The boat looked empty. A small runabout with a powerful outboard engine was tied at the stern. The scuba gear Olivia had noticed earlier was in the smaller boat.

Olivia opened her mouth to say something. Just then, a tall man with a scruffy blond beard stepped out of the cabin onto the boat's aft deck. "What do you two want?"

"We're on the sailboat over there." I pointed. "*Jeopardy*. We just thought we'd say hi."

"Uh-huh. Well, we're not exactly the Welcome Wagon here." He frowned.

I shrugged. "That's all right; we're just going ashore anyway."

Olivia shaded her eyes from the sun and looked up at the bearded man. "I noticed the dive gear in your runabout...what are you diving for?"

His face suddenly changed, eyes narrowing and mouth becoming a tight line beneath the blond mustache. He stepped backward and folded his arms across his chest. "None of your business, kid."

"Hey," I protested. "She was just making conversation."

"Yeah? Well, like I said, we're not the Welcome Wagon. I don't have time for this."

He turned away and stepped into the darkness of the cabin.

So much for being polite to the neighbors. "All right then," I drawled. I pushed our dinghy away from the boat and looked at Olivia with raised eyebrows.

She was nodding, like the man had just confirmed something she'd suspected all along. "I can't believe it," she whispered.

I started to row. "What? That they aren't the Welcome Wagon?"

She gave me a green-eyed stare. "They're hiding something."

"You don't know that," I scoffed. "Maybe he liked having the bay to himself and is annoyed that we anchored here too. Maybe he hates teenagers. Maybe he's just a jerk."

Olivia leaned toward me, and her black hair hung forward, covering one eye. The other eye looked at me fiercely. "No way," she said. "Didn't you see what was on the deck?"

chapter five

I looked back at the cabin cruiser. I couldn't
see anything out of the ordinary: just some
storage bins, a bucket and some rope. The
usual kind of boat clutter. "What?" I asked.
"What did you see?"

"Shells," Olivia whispered.

"Shells. You mean shells from a gun?" I
wasn't actually quite sure what that meant.
Bullet casings or something. I wouldn't know
one if I tripped over it.

She gave me the kind of look people usually give me before they call me Spacey. "No, Simon. Shells like in seashells."

"Uh-huh." She really was nuts. "And what, you think they're making decorations or something? Shell nightlights, maybe, or shell ashtrays?" I laughed. "Okay, that stuff is so ugly that maybe it ought to be illegal, but..."

She kicked me. "Simon. I think they're poaching abalone."

"Ouch." I pulled my legs out of her reach. "Abalone?"

"It's a shellfish. People eat it—"

"Yeah, I know. Like clams."

"Except that there's been a total ban on taking abalone from around here for years."

I shook my head. It didn't sound like that big a deal to me. Who cared if these guys ate a few fish? "How come you know all this?" I asked.

"Dad's so-called student did some research on abalone and told me all about it." She scowled. "Before I knew she was sleeping with him."

"Huh."

Olivia glanced toward shore. Then she turned and looked over to *Jeopardy.* "I think we should go back and tell Patrick."

"What's he going to do?"

"Call and report it."

I stopped rowing for a moment and stretched out my legs. "Can't it wait?" I was dying to walk a bit. Hauling up sails and working those winches is a great upper body workout, and keeping your balance on a boat that is rolling and pounding in the waves uses muscles you didn't know you had. Still, after being on the boat all day, my legs were stiff and cramped.

Olivia hesitated. She looked out at the cabin cruiser. In the early evening light, its white hull gleamed against the dark water. "I guess they're not going anywhere."

"Nah, they wouldn't want to leave their abalone." I grinned to let her know I was just kidding.

She didn't grin back. "You don't believe me, do you?"

I shrugged. "I don't know. It just seems a bit unlikely. There are lots of other reasons they could be diving. And a few shells on the deck...well, lots of people pick up shells."

Olivia's eyes were icy. "Fine," she said. "I'll talk to Patrick about it, and we'll see what he says."

We walked along the shore in silence for a while, but it wasn't the friendly silence that we'd had earlier. I thought about apologizing, but I didn't see why I should. She was just making a huge deal out of what was probably nothing at all.

When we got back to our boat, Patrick, Joey and Blair were all down below playing cards. Olivia didn't even say hello before she launched into her story. She stood there, her hands on her skinny hips and her black hair all wild from the dinghy ride, and started ranting about endangered abalone and poaching and scuba gear.

Patrick listened with an amused half smile. Finally he held up one hand. "Hold on there, Olivia. Are you serious? You think the men on the boat over there are doing something illegal? Just because they have scuba gear?"

He made it sound ridiculous, and even though I agreed with him, I couldn't help feeling bad for Olivia.

She nodded and folded her arms across her chest defensively. "And shells on their deck. Yes."

Joey laughed. "Man, don't tell me you're one of those conspiracy theorists. Hey, Olivia, do you think Princess Diana faked her own death?"

She gave him a withering look and didn't bother to respond. "Patrick...look, my dad's a marine biologist. I do actually know something about this and I'm pretty sure I saw shucked abalone shells on that boat."

Patrick sighed and climbed the companionway steps, sticking his head out the hatch and looking over toward the cabin cruiser. He pulled a pack of cigarettes out of his pocket and lit one. "Listen, honey..."

"Olivia."

"Olivia, then. I really doubt they're doing anything they shouldn't be doing, but if it'll make you feel better, I'll go over there and have a word with them."

"Great. Great." Olivia sat down at the table with Blair and Joey. "Thanks, Patrick. I mean, I hope I'm wrong, but I'd feel much better if you checked it out."

He winked. "No problem."

Patrick got in the dinghy and set off, the thrum of the engine jarring in the quiet anchorage.

Blair shook his head at Olivia. "That was a good game of cards you just interrupted."

"So excuse me for thinking that a threatened species is slightly more important than a game of...what, Crazy Eights?"

"Poker. And I had a full house." He tossed his cards on the table and ran his hands through his blond-highlighted hair. "Anyway, it's just a freaking fish. I mean, okay, if it was baby seals or something..."

Olivia looked furious. "I hate how people only care about animals that are cute. Anyway, it's not a fish. It's a marine mollusc."

Blair started laughing. "Mollusc," he said, like it was the funniest thing he'd ever heard. Joey punched his brother on the shoulder and joined in, snorting loudly and spluttering his Coke everywhere. "Mollusc."

"A mollusc is a shellfish," Olivia said coldly. "Abalone is a univalve mollusc, meaning it has a single part shell—not two parts joined together like a clam."

Blair and Joey started laughing even harder. A fine spray of Joey's Coke settled on my glasses. Nice. I'd dreamed about this trip for months and here I was, stuck on a boat with a shellfish-obsessed girl and two junior yacht clubbers whose combined IQ was probably less than that of a...mollusc.

chapter six

We had all drifted outside and were sitting in the cockpit, slapping at mosquitoes and watching dark clouds forming along the horizon when Patrick returned. He'd been gone for a while: the man in the cabin cruiser must have been a bit friendlier to him than he'd been to us.

"Well, you can all relax," he told us as he climbed the stern ladder and stepped aboard. "No small sea creatures are having their rights violated."

Olivia tilted her head back and looked up at him searchingly. "So, what are those men doing here then?"

"Those men are Keith and Victor. They're just enjoying the scenery. All right?" He laughed. "The only crime they're committing is cruising on that diesel-guzzling stinkpot instead of a sailboat."

"And the dive gear?" Olivia asked stubbornly.

"There're some wrecks nearby. They're divers. Like I said, they're just checking out the local scenery." Patrick grinned. Olivia almost smiled. Then he flicked his cigarette butt into the water, and Olivia's mouth opened in a horrified circle. For a second I thought she might jump overboard to retrieve it, but instead she just stood up, turned and disappeared down below into the cabin.

"Man, there goes a girl who hates to be wrong," Patrick said.

We all laughed, but I felt a pang of guilt and hoped she hadn't heard him. Olivia was definitely a sore loser, but she was the only one who hadn't called me Spacey.

Patrick looked out at the clouds. "Doesn't look good," he said. "Wind's picking up too."

I hadn't noticed, but he was right. A strong breeze was starting to whistle through the rigging, and the water was no longer smooth as glass.

"This anchorage should be okay," Patrick said. "We might have a bit of an uncomfortable night, but it'll be safe enough." He rubbed his cheeks and chin thoughtfully. "Not sure about tomorrow though. If this keeps up we won't be able to cross the Nawetti Bar."

"We're going to a bar?" Joey asked hopefully.

Patrick chuckled. "The Nawetti Bar. It's a stretch where the water suddenly gets shallower, which creates all kinds of currents and nasty sailing conditions. It's a tricky bit of water, but we have to cross it to get around Cape Scott." He shrugged. "Often boats have to wait here a few days to get the right weather. I'd hoped we'd get lucky and go early tomorrow at slack tide, but...well, let's listen to the weather."

He switched the VHF radio onto the marine weather channel. I tried to listen, but the monotone voice of the weather guy was putting me to sleep. I found myself thinking about my dad and how he didn't want me to sail, and Olivia, whose dad was making her learn even though she couldn't care less. Fathers were strange. Why couldn't they just accept their kids as they were?

"Earth to Spacey!" Joey yelled, snapping me back to the present.

"Sorry," I muttered. "What?"

"We're gonna have another game of poker. You want to play?"

I shook my head. "Think I'll read a bit," I told him.

"Come on," Patrick kidded me. "Team player, remember?"

I glanced up at them all. Joey and Blair had changed into expensive-looking fleece jackets and were lounging in the cockpit as if they were posing for an ad in a glossy cruising magazine. "Not tonight, thanks. I'm beat," I said. Then I grabbed the cruising guide and headed for my berth to read about where we were going.

The wind picked up overnight, howling through the rigging loudly enough to wake me. The boat bounced gently up and down. I looked at my watch: 4:00 AM. Ugh. I closed my eyes but couldn't get back to sleep. The motion started to make me a little queasy—not really sick, just sort of drooly and drugged. I wanted to get up and move around, but there was nowhere to go. I wanted off the boat or out of my body, and neither seemed very likely. I wondered if anyone else was awake.

What I'd read last night about the Nawetti Bar and Cape Scott pretty much confirmed what Patrick had said. Unless the wind suddenly dropped, I didn't think we'd be going anywhere in the morning. Stuck here with this group...what a freaking nightmare. Single-handed sailing was sounding better all the time. I imagined myself setting sail across the turquoise waters of the Caribbean, alone on a luxury boat. A sixty-foot Swan, say...with roller-furling sails and self-tailing winches and a huge cockpit with a large stainless steel wheel and...

I guess I must have drifted off to sleep, because next thing I knew Patrick was yelling at us all to rise and shine. As soon as I opened my eyes, the nausea returned. And it was barely even light out. Ugh.

"Blair and Joey are making pancakes," Patrick said. "Mmmm..."

Olivia stumbled out to the table in blue flannel pajamas. She tugged a black sweatshirt over her head. "I'm flipping starving," she announced. "Bring 'em on."

I guessed no one else was feeling seasick. I dragged myself out to the table. "Morning."

"You're looking a little rough there, Simon," Patrick said. "You sleep okay?"

"Fine." I sat there in grumpy silence for a few minutes. I'd read that seasickness was usually worst for the first few days. I sure hoped that was true, because if it didn't get better, my plan to be a delivery skipper was looking a little shaky. Anyway, being upright seemed to help, and by the time Joey was flipping steaming pancakes out of the frying pan, I was actually feeling almost hungry.

"Here you go, Mollusc girl." Joey flipped a few pancakes onto Olivia's plate. "Eat up. It might be the only vegetarian meal of the day."

Olivia ignored him and began eating. After putting away three enormous pancakes, she put her fork down and looked at Patrick. "You know, I've been thinking about last night..."

"Uh-huh?" Patrick took a swig of his coffee and winced. "Man, that was hot."

"I think those men were lying to you."

He groaned. "Here we go again."

"I'm serious. If they were just diving on wrecks, why were they so unfriendly? Besides, what about the shells I saw on their boat? I'm almost certain they were abalone."

"Well, what do you want me to do, Olivia? Send off some flares?"

She hesitated. "Can't you call someone on the radio?"

He laughed. "Sure. The range is maybe twenty miles at best. Odds are the only people that will hear us are the two guys on that boat."

"Well, there must be something we can do." Olivia scowled. "We can't go today anyway, right? So I'm going to row over there again and get another look at those shells."

"Not a good idea," Patrick said, shaking his head. "If those guys are poachers, the last thing you want to do is go poking around."

"You think they'd be dangerous?" Joey sounded disbelieving.

"If they were poaching abalone and they were caught, yeah. They'd have a lot to lose." Patrick was answering Joey, but his eyes were fixed on Olivia.

"But—," she started to protest.

He shook his head. "I mean it, Olivia. You'd be best to just mind your own business and stay out of their way."

"I can't do that," Olivia burst out. "If they're doing something that actually threatens the survival of a species—"

"Mollusc," Blair said, and he and Joey started laughing.

"Drop it, Olivia," Patrick ordered. "I'd hate to see anything happen to you."

I could tell by the set of Olivia's jaw that she wasn't going to drop it. It wasn't in that girl's nature to drop anything. There was a long silence, or at least as much of a silence as there could be with the wind howling. Finally Patrick sighed. "Get everything well stowed," he said. "I think we'd better head out this morning after all."

chapter seven

To borrow my dad's expression, the wind was strong enough to blow dogs off chains.

Up at the mast, I unzipped the sail cover and unfastened the ties that held it in place; then I pulled it off to uncover the main-sail, still securely tied around the boom. The wind tried to rip the cover from my hands as I bundled it up and stowed it in a cockpit locker. The sky was just getting light, a streak of white staining the dark gray horizon.

Olivia, Joey and Blair huddled under the dodger as we motored out of the anchorage. Patrick was at the helm, his face grim. I stood beside him, waiting to take the helm. He'd told us that I would take the first watch and that Olivia could navigate. Of course, he was watching and supervising, but he'd only step in if we needed him to.

After what I'd read last night, I couldn't believe we were leaving Bull Harbour in this weather. I listened to Patrick telling Joey and Blair to raise the sails, and I wondered what he was thinking. Obviously, he knew these waters a lot better than any of us did. He wouldn't take us out there if he didn't think it was going to be safe. Or would he?

Twenty minutes later, I was hanging onto that wheel as if it were a life ring and concentrating on keeping the pancakes down. Beside me, Olivia's face had taken on a greenish tinge. Patrick and Blair were up at the mast, shortening the mainsail with a second reef and Joey was down below.

His response to seasickness seemed to be to go to sleep.

"This is pretty intense." Olivia spoke like she was trying to sound casual, but her voice sounded tight and about an octave higher than usual.

The wind was a shrieking monster behind us, and *Jeopardy* was barely in control, surfing down steep waves with an eerie roar as the water rushed under its hull. Every so often, a wave came at us beam on—sideways—rolling us dangerously to one side. I'd been out in all kinds of weather, but I'd never seen waves as steep as these. "It's nuts," I said flatly. I raised my voice so that she'd be able to hear me over the screaming wind and the crashing water. "And it's only going to get worse. I don't think we're even on the bar yet. We shouldn't be out here."

"I guess Patrick knows what he's doing," she shouted back.

"Uh-huh." I watched our instructor up at the mast, wrestling with the sail. He was shouting orders to Blair, but the wind snatched his words and carried them away.

"I don't know."

"What?"

"Well, I just wondered about what he said this morning. I got the impression we weren't going anywhere until you brought up the abalone thing." I glanced sideways at her. "He seemed worried."

She scowled and spat out her words. "That's stupid."

"Yeah, I know...but what if he suspected you were right about the guys on that cabin cruiser? You know, he was over there. Maybe he saw something odd." I hesitated, not wanting to sound like I was criticizing him, and then I went on. "I don't think we should have left Bull Harbour today."

"I guess he's got a bit more experience than you," Olivia snapped. "He's sailed around Vancouver Island dozens of times."

I stared at her, taken aback by her tone. "You have a thing for older men or something?" I guessed Patrick would be considered good looking, but Olivia did nothing but argue with him.

"Don't be an idiot, Simon." Olivia stared down at the chart, avoiding my eyes. "I just think he probably knows what he's doing." Her cheeks were pink.

I started to laugh. "You're blushing, Olivia. Admit it, you like him."

"Shut up," she said coldly. "Just shut up. Go back to whatever little dream world you live in." She moved away from me and sat down under the dodger, bracing one foot on the wooden edge of the companionway.

"Hey...Olivia..."

She ignored me and stared off at the horizon, her black hair blowing everywhere. Her cheeks were wet, but I couldn't tell whether from spray or tears. Probably spray. She didn't seem the type to cry.

Up at the mast, Blair and Patrick finally managed to tie a second reef in the mainsail. It slowed us down a little, but we were still hurtling along with the wind behind us. The sky was a heavy gray, with banks of darker clouds hanging ominously over the horizon. The wind was blowing the tops off the waves, and there was so much spray it was hard to see where we were going.

I thought about what I'd read last night. The cruising guide strongly suggested waiting for calm conditions before crossing the Nawetti Bar. If the conditions weren't perfect—which to me sounded like slack tide and no wind at all—it could be one of the most dangerous places around. Boats a hundred feet long have been sunk in these waters, the guide book had said. I wondered if we were there yet, or if things were going to get even worse. "Where are we?" I shouted to Olivia. "How far have we gone?"

She shrugged sullenly. "I don't have a freaking clue. Every time I try to look at the chart, I start feeling sick. It's worse than reading in a car, and I can't do that either."

We were supposed to be using dead reckoning to navigate—keeping track of our speed and compass course, and using a pencil to mark our position on the chart. I was a bit shaky on all of that. Besides, if you actually took the chart out of its plastic case, it'd get

51

soaked. "Forget the chart then," I yelled. "Are you using the GPS?"

Olivia held up the little electronic device. "I can't get a fix with the GPS. It's not working."

"What do you mean?" I couldn't help feeling a bit panicky, although I knew Patrick was probably keeping track of everything anyway. I looked over to see him and Blair heading back to the cockpit, bodies crouching low for balance and hands clutching railings and rigging as they made their way along the slippery deck.

"The little screen just keeps saying that it can't get a clear satellite signal." She looked up at the sky. "Maybe it's too cloudy."

I snorted. "That's not much use then, is it?" I stared into the spray and wished glasses came with little windshield wipers. "I can't see a thing."

"Believe me, you don't want to." Olivia wrapped her arms around herself and shuddered. "Simon, I don't like this."

"Look, I'm sure..." I was about to say something reassuring about boats floating like ducks and Patrick knowing what he was doing, but a huge wave rose up beside us, lifting the starboard side of the boat so steeply I actually thought we might get knocked down. I gasped as Patrick grabbed the wheel from me and turned the boat away from the wave. *Jeopardy*'s stern lifted, and we leveled out slightly; then the bow dropped as we surfed crazily with the breaking wave. I took the wheel back, my hands shaking and my heart pounding. That had been way too close.

"Woo-hoo!" Blair shouted. He sat down beside Olivia. "This is awesome."

I guess being totally clueless has its advantages. Blair didn't seem to have any idea that these weren't ideal sailing conditions. Nor, I noted jealously, did he seem to be getting sick. "Here you go, cowboy," I told him. "You take the helm." Then I leaned over the port-side rail, which was almost buried in the waves anyway, and threw up.

Patrick leaned close and spoke softly in my ear as I stood back up. "Well, Spacey, at least you remembered to heave your guts downwind. Nothing worse than having it fly back at you." He laughed and wiped his dripping nose with the back of his hand.

I didn't say anything. I was starting to think our instructor was as crazy as the crew.

He stepped back. "Look," he said loudly, looking around to make sure we were all listening. "That wave back there...you can't take those on the beam. You see a really big wave coming, you gotta steer. A wave like that can knock a boat right down on its side and do some real damage."

"Maybe we should turn back," Olivia said.

I agreed with her, but I didn't say anything. I wanted to do well in this course, and I didn't want Patrick to think I was scared of heavy-weather sailing. If I was going to be a long-distance sailor, I'd be out at sea for weeks at a time. I wouldn't get to choose my weather.

Patrick hesitated. He looked at the jagged line of the horizon and blew out a long breath. Then he shook his head. "We'll keep going."

chapter eight

I didn't know time could move so slowly. Every wave was a lifetime, every pause between waves just long enough to catch your breath and brace yourself for the next one.

There was no thinking, no talking, nothing but noise and water and wind.

It was a roller-coaster ride and just like on a roller coaster, the worst part was that moment when you hung suspended at the peak, waiting for the inevitable plummeting rush down the other side. The only difference was that this ride went on and on, and it had stopped being fun a long time ago. I tried to imagine that I was alone at sea, sailing my boat through a tropical storm, days from land. It didn't help.

When I glanced at my watch, only five minutes had passed since we came close to being knocked down. After that happened, Patrick insisted that we all strap ourselves into safety harnesses. They reminded me of those chest harnesses people sometimes put on dogs or toddlers. They fit snugly over our life jackets and rain gear and had six-foot leashes attached to them. The leashes clipped on to thick stainless-steel bolts in the cockpit, the idea being that whatever happened, no one could be swept off the boat. I remembered the man-overboard drill with a shudder. In these conditions, if someone went over, getting them back on the boat would be impossible. If someone went over, they were as good as dead. I tried not to think about it and tightened my safety harness.

Patrick was at the helm. Olivia and I were taking turns holding each other's ankles while the other one heaved over the side of the boat. Blair was still hollering like a cowboy, and Joey hadn't appeared from down below. It occurred to me that someone should probably check on him.

"Blair!" I yelled. "Is Joey all right?"

"I'll go see." He clambered awkwardly down the companionway, swearing as his leash caught him short and pausing to unclip it before descending into the cabin.

Olivia looked at me miserably. "This is all my fault," she said.

"What are you talking about?" The boat lurched down another watery cliff, and we both braced our feet against the opposite side of the cockpit and hung on.

"What you said before—you were right."

I could feel my eyebrows shooting up my forehead. I leaned closer to her so I wouldn't have to shout over the wind. Standing behind the big wheel, Patrick was only a few feet away. "About you having a crush on Patrick?"

"No, dope. About his judgement being off." She looked at me anxiously. "He didn't want us to hang around Bull Harbour, because he didn't trust me not to snoop around that boat."

"Well..." I couldn't help thinking that hanging around with possible poachers sounded like a picnic compared with being out here.

"He decided it was safer to leave. And now..." She looked out at the endless stretch of heaving gray water, and her voice got so quiet I could hardly hear it over the wind. "Now we're out here, and it's my fault."

"That's stupid," I said. "Patrick is the captain. It's his job to decide what weather conditions are safe. If it's anyone's fault, it's his."

She shook her head. "I hate sailing."

Blair's head poked up from down below. He hung onto both sides of the companionway and, with a jerk of his chin, motioned for us to come closer. "Joey won't get up," he said. "He keeps saying he needs to sleep."

"You think he's okay?" I asked.

"I think he took too much Gravol."

"Too much? Like, an overdose?" That was all we needed.

"Nah. Like two or three. The stuff just knocks him out."

Olivia looked worried. "I think we should tell Patrick."

"He's just a lazy bugger," Blair said.

I swallowed and tasted vomit. Seasickness sucked. "Got any more of that Gravol?" I asked.

Blair nodded and disappeared. A minute later, he handed up two tablets. I swallowed them dry and almost immediately threw them back up again.

I looked up to see Patrick watching. With one hand on the wheel, a grin on his suntanned face and his shoulders broad in his foul-weather jacket, he looked just how I wanted to look. Instead, I was hunched over miserably, wiping my mouth and wishing I was anywhere else.

He cocked his head to one side and winked at me. "Hang in there, Simon. It'll get better. You know, some of the best sailors get seasick."

I nodded. "Okay."

"Here, take the helm. It'll help." Patrick stepped to one side, and I moved into his place, taking the wheel. "Trying to focus on anything close will make it worse, so don't stare at the compass or the sails. Just glance at them if you need to and then look at the horizon."

I nodded and squinted through wet salt-speckled lenses. "Thanks."

"You don't give up easy," Patrick said. "I like that."

As we headed northwest, the waves got steeper. Blair threw up, which made me feel slightly better, and Patrick started to look worried.

"I want to go back," Olivia said. "This is awful."

Patrick frowned. "It's not good," he admitted.

"So, can we turn around?" Blair asked hopefully.

I held my breath. I wanted to go back, but I didn't want to admit it. I was still feeling good about Patrick saying that I didn't give up easily. I wasn't going to give him reason to change his mind.

He hesitated. "Let's give it a few more minutes. If the wind doesn't let up, we'll turn around."

Joey, Blair and Olivia all cheered. I looked behind us, in the direction of Bull Harbour, and thought I understood Patrick's hesitation. Turning around would mean sailing into the wind, instead of running from it. Turning around was not going to be pleasant.

Then a huge wave appeared beneath us. A solid gray wall of water. A monster of a wave, twice the size of the rest, lifting us up. That roller-coaster moment of hanging at the top. Then the rushing down, the roar of water, and the stern of the boat suddenly slewing to starboard so that *Jeopardy* was beam on to the monster wave.

Patrick cursed and grabbed the wheel from me, trying to bring *Jeopardy* back under control and straighten it up. I dove forward to release the main sheet, unsure if it was the right thing to do but knowing I had to do something.

But it was too late. It happened so fast, there was barely time to blink. *Jeopardy* was slammed onto its side, and we were thrown down and plunged into the icy water.

chapter nine

"This is it," I thought as the water roared into the cockpit. "We're going to die."

It seemed so strange that death could happen just like that. I felt oddly calm. My heart was beating slowly: thump, thump, thump. Around me was a sudden quiet filled with cold water and confusion. Then my head began to clear, and the world around me began to make sense again.

Jeopardy was lying on its side, its mast in the water and the deck half buried. Not moving. Dead in the water. I was standing on what used to be a vertical surface—the side of the cockpit bench. The others were all still there, looking shell-shocked, clinging to stanchions and to the rigging. *Jeopardy* was struggling, trying to right itself. It couldn't, because the sails were submerged, and the weight of water was holding it pinned to the waves.

I crawled forward along the deck to the base of the mast, released the main halyard to free the sail and began pulling the sodden canvas out of the water and onto the part of the deck that was still visible. Patrick appeared beside me, and then Joey. Working together, we managed to get the mainsail out of the water and lashed to the boom.

Jeopardy started to rise, battling its way out of the water and turning into the wind. I couldn't help cheering. What a boat. To take a blow like that and come up fighting... For some reason, I suddenly thought of my dad. I wanted to tell him about this, to make him understand that sailing was about more than lounging in fancy marinas. I wanted to tell him that this was more exciting, more challenging—more real—than any football game.

I hoped I was going to have the chance.

Olivia was at the helm, holding the wheel with a huge grin. Happy to be alive, I figured, grinning back at her a little crazily. I was sopping wet, water cascading down my arms and back inside my rain gear. High above the deck, *Jeopardy*'s port-side spreader was broken, dangling forlornly from the mast. Blair was cradling one arm against his side and wincing. But *Jeopardy*, still flying a small triangle of jib sail, was bravely upright and sailing close to the wind, back in the general direction of Bull Harbour.

Patrick took the wheel from Olivia and began barking orders at us. We all leapt to obey, relieved and grateful to have him assume control.

"Who's got first-aid training?" he yelled above the wind.

Olivia raised her hand like we were in a classroom.

"Okay. Take Blair down below, give him some ibuprofen and make a sling for his arm."

"Fell against the bulkhead when the boat went over," Blair explained. "Sorry guys." Looking embarrassed, he followed Olivia through the companionway and down into the cabin.

Patrick turned to Joey. "The port-side spreader's broken," he shouted, pointing up at the dangling metal arm halfway up the mast. "So what kind of problem do you think that leaves us with?"

Joey shook his head. "Look, man, you don't have to be the instructor right now. Just tell us what to do." His face was white and he looked terrified.

"The mast is unstable," I said. "Without the spreader to hold the tension on the rigging, the mast isn't balanced properly."

"That's the right answer," Patrick said. "But I wasn't asking you. I was asking Joey."

"I was just trying to help. I thought you wanted me to be a team player."

"Well, you and Joey can work together to secure the mast," he said. "We'll have to head back to Bull Harbour under power." He started up the engine and *Jeopardy* began motoring directly into the steep waves. No more surfing downwind—now we were pounding along, banging into the breaking waves. It felt like speeding down a rutted, potholed road in a car with no shocks. We hit each wave with a shuddering crash, and I had to bend my knees to absorb the impact.

"Wouldn't it be better just to keep going?" I asked. "I mean, we must be pretty close to being over the bar, right?"

Patrick shook his head. "Cape Scott wouldn't be a picnic either. Even I'm not crazy enough to attempt that with broken rigging." He brushed his wet hair away from his eyes. "Much as I hate to admit it, we have to go back."

I nodded and studied the rigging. There was only one obvious way to secure the mast and that was to use a halyard. I looked at Joey. "If we fasten the extra jib halyard to the toe rail, it'll help support the mast."

He just stared at me blankly.

"Joey...you okay, man?" I wondered if he'd hit his head when we got knocked down.

"I just went flying out of that berth. I opened my eyes, and everything was the wrong way up, and water was pouring in." He gazed out at the waves around us. "I thought we were gonna die. You know?"

I did know, but I didn't really want to think about it. "Yeah, well, we're okay now," I said. "So, come on, let's do it. I'll get the halyard."

"Halyard," he echoed.

"Yeah. You know. The rope that runs up the inside of the mast and out the top? We use it to raise and lower the sail?" I was starting to feel a bit worried. It was shock, I thought, but wrapping him in warm blankets or whatever it is you're supposed to do wasn't really an option right now. I kept talking to him instead. "Okay, Joey? Come on. We can do it together. Here..." I crept forward and unclipped the stainless-steel shackle from the starboard-side toe rail, so that the halyard hung free from the top of the mast. "Take it, Joey."

Joey took it.

"Now fasten it to the toe rail on your side," I told him, watching carefully. He was moving slowly and wasn't talking much, but he seemed okay.

I wrapped the other end of the halyard around the winch on the mast; then I grabbed a winch handle and started to crank the halyard tight. It was hard to know how much pressure to put on it. I wanted the tension on the port side to be as close as possible to the tension held by the rigging on the starboard side. I looked up at the mast but from my position at the base, it was difficult to judge.

I glanced at Patrick again, wondering whether to ask him if the mast looked straight from his perspective at the helm, but I was still stinging from his earlier rebuke. "What do you think, Joey?" I yelled. "Does the mast look straight?"

Joey stood in the cockpit, holding onto the dodger for balance. The color was returning to his face. "It looks good," he shouted back.

I nodded. Kneeling on the cabin roof, I tied the halyard to a cleat on the mast. I was just starting to get up when *Jeopardy* crashed into a wave with a bone-jarring, tooth-rattling jolt. I actually felt myself lift up, getting a couple of seconds of airtime before smashing back down. Cursing and rubbing my bruised knees, I made my way back to the cockpit.

Olivia and Blair emerged from down below. Olivia looked slightly green, and Blair's arm was in a neatly tied sling.

"Hey there, Nurse Olivia," I teased.

Olivia narrowed her eyes at me and turned away to throw up over the railing.

I sat down and the rest of the gang gradually joined me, all hunched as close to the dodger as possible. Every wave we hit sent a sheet of icy water cascading into the cockpit. I stuck my head through the companionway and peeked down into the cabin. Everything was sopping wet—bedding, carpet, charts. Water must have been pouring into the cabin when we were knocked down. I could hear the steady hum of the electric bilge pump over the noise of the engine. We were going to have a huge mess to clean up when we got back to Bull Harbour.

Now that the adrenalin was wearing off, I was feeling queasy again. I shuffled my butt along the bench and leaned back to look at the line of the horizon. The wind was still howling furiously, and beside me, Olivia was shivering so hard I could hear her teeth chattering.

"At least it'd be warm in the Caribbean," I told her.

"If we ever actually make it back to land," Olivia said darkly, "I am never getting on another boat again." She stared at me, her wet hair plastered to her scalp. "Why would any sane person choose to do this?"

I had to admit she had a point.

chapter ten

It took forever to get back to Bull Harbour. Now that we were motoring into the wind, instead of sailing with it behind us, the motion was different. Gone was the roar and whoosh of surfing down the waves, just on the edge of control. Now we pounded along, each wave almost bringing *Jeopardy* to a jarring halt. The engine was loud, and we were cold, wet, sick and miserable. Patrick made a few feeble attempts to turn the experience into a lesson on heavy-weather sailing, but no one was in the mood. After a while he just gave up and sat by himself, smoking with his hand cupped around his cigarette and looking out to sea.

It was still morning when we finally got back into Bull Harbour, but it felt like a lifetime ago that we'd left. The wind had dropped to fifteen knots, just a decent sailing breeze, and the water in the bay was calm. Joey and I lowered the anchor, more or less in the same spot we'd been the previous night. *Salty Mist* was still there, and I wondered whether that boat was really the reason we had left. It was hard to imagine that those men posed any danger that even came close to what we'd just experienced.

Patrick put the engine in reverse to set the anchor; then he hit the off switch, and the anchorage was quiet and peaceful again.

"I'm starving," Olivia said explosively. "Absolutely starving."

My stomach growled and I realized we hadn't eaten anything since that morning's pancakes. "Me too. What's for lunch?"

Patrick laughed. "Okay. Dry clothes if you can find any, then we'll get some food and deal with everything else afterward. Sound like a plan?"

It did. We all descended into the cabin in search of clothing that wasn't completely saturated and found that of the four of us, only Blair and Joey still had dry bags. A few minutes later, all four of us were dressed like junior yacht clubbers. My dad would have laughed his head off. Of course, their clothes were enormous on Olivia and me—the pants I was wearing were about a foot longer than my legs, and Olivia had pretty much disappeared inside a huge navy blue sweater. I didn't care. It just felt good to be warm and dry.

Patrick puttered around on the deck, checking for damage and tidying up. Blair and Joey found a shepherd's pie in the freezer and set it on the table while they tried to get the oven working. An unusual meal for mid-morning, but it sounded great to me. My mouth watered. I spread a garbage bag over the damp berth and sat down on it.

Olivia looked at the long list of ingredients on the cardboard package and made a face. She sighed and rummaged in the lockers until she found a bag of peanuts. Then she sat down beside me and tipped some nuts straight into her mouth. Turning, she offered me the bag.

I crammed a handful of peanuts into my own mouth and sighed with pleasure. "Mmmm...thanks."

She chewed, swallowed and wiped her mouth with the back of her hand. "You know what the best thing is?"

"Yeah. Food."

"No, stupid. That we're still alive. Seriously. When the boat went over like that, I thought we were history."

"I know." I licked the salt off my fingers and tipped some more nuts into my palm. "I was pretty happy to see Bull Harbour again."

Olivia nodded. "Me too." Her eyes suddenly widened. "You know what?"

"What?"

"We're going to get another chance to find out what's going on with that boat."

She lowered her voice to a whisper. "The poachers."

I stared at her incredulously. "You have got to be kidding. Patrick isn't going to let us near them."

"We don't have to tell him. I've got it all figured out. We wait until the others are in bed. Then we take the dinghy over. If I could just get a closer look at those shells, I'd know for sure."

I shook my head. "I think I've had enough excitement for one day."

"They won't even know we're there. I'll just take a couple of those shucked shells, and when we get to a port, I'll make a phone call. That's it." She looked at me imploringly. "Please?"

Her hands kept disappearing inside her sleeves, which were so long they dangled loosely from the ends of her arms. I took my glasses off and rubbed them on my sweater. "How come I'm part of your plan?"

"The others would just laugh. You pretend you don't care about the abalone, but I know you do."

"Yeah, sort of. If it's a threatened species, no one should be trying to make a buck off them." I noticed the smile that flashed across her face and I shook my head quickly. "I'm not saying I'll do it. I think Patrick's right. Going over to that boat isn't such a great idea."

Olivia's still damp hair stuck out wildly, and Blair's enormous sweater made her look about twelve. She looked down at the floor and sighed. "Will you think about it?" she asked.

I nodded.

Patrick clambered down the steps into the cabin. "Lunch almost ready?"

Blair shook his head. "Can't get the oven working. Anyone feel like cheese sandwiches?" He slid some plates across the smooth wooden table and dumped a loaf of bread in the middle.

Patrick stripped off his wet jacket and sweater and sat down at the table in his damp T-shirt. "The stove isn't the only problem. We've got a broken spreader, plus all the battens in the mainsail are broken." He rubbed his hands over his cheeks and rested his elbows on the table. "It looks like we're going to have to do some repairs before we head north again. We're going to have to go back to Port Hardy."

We all looked at him and at each other. "Man," Joey groaned. "That sucks."

"No kidding," Blair agreed. "We were supposed to go surfing in Tofino."

"What about the course?" I asked. "I need to get this qualification."

Patrick shrugged. "We can do day sails from Port Hardy. There's other boats. We'll work something out."

I didn't want to do day sails. I wanted the full-on, live-aboard, cruising experience. But at least I still had a shot at getting my Intermediate Cruising qualification.

Olivia was the only one who looked happy. "If we get to Port Hardy, I'm checking into a hotel," she declared.

Patrick rested his head in his hands. He looked exhausted. "I'm sorry about all this," he said. "I misjudged the conditions today. We shouldn't have been out there."

There was an awkward silence as we all silently agreed with him.

Blair finally broke it. "Whatever. I'm starving. Let's eat."

Patrick went into the head to change into dry clothes—apparently he stored some of his things in giant Zip-lock bags. I mentally filed that idea for future reference. While Blair and Joey put a brick of cheese and a few tomatoes on the table, Olivia whispered to me, "If you won't come with me tonight, I'm going on my own."

I looked at her, and she looked steadily back, her eyes full of challenge. "I'll come," I told her.

She grinned. "I knew you would."

chapter eleven

I lay in my damp coffin berth, with my borrowed jeans and sweatshirt still on, and wondered why I'd agreed to go. Curiousity, mostly, and not liking the idea of Olivia going out alone in the dinghy at night.

Odds were we'd get over there, and she'd see that those shells were really just a few empty oyster shells they'd picked up to use as ashtrays or something. Olivia was pretty confident, but her dad was a marine biologist, so of course she thought she was an expert on shellfish. Molluscs. Back home, I knew a kid whose mom was a singer, and he considered himself the authority on everything to do with the music industry.

I stifled an urge to laugh and realized I was getting nervous. What if Olivia was right? Patrick's decision to leave Bull Harbour in such dangerous conditions was odd—he was too experienced a sailor to make that kind of error. Had he really thought that the men on the cruiser could be dangerous? My stomach twisted as I remembered what he had said: *I'd hate to see anything happen to you.*

The boat was silent. I looked at my watch. Midnight. Across the cabin, I could hear someone snoring softly. Patrick, I thought. It was now or never. I slipped out of my berth and tiptoed over to Olivia's. If anyone woke up, I'd just pretend I was on my way to the head. In the inky darkness, no one could see that I was fully dressed.

"Olivia?" I whispered.

"Ready?"

"I guess." I couldn't make out her face, just a faint outline moving in the blackness.

We crept across the cabin and slid open the companionway boards, careful not to make a sound. Then we slipped out into the cockpit and into the night.

The winds had blown the clouds from the sky, and a pale moon hung low, illuminating the harbor like an enormous lantern. The wind blew briskly, rattling loose halyards and sending small waves skimming across the water. A couple of hundred feet away, *Salty Mist*'s outline was just visible in the moonlight, and its anchor light glowed softly.

"Perfect night for a bit of snooping," Olivia whispered. "I brought a flashlight, but the moon is so bright, I don't think we'll need it."

I nodded. "And it's good that it's a bit windy. It'll help cover any noise we make."

Olivia pulled on the tow rope that attached the dinghy to *Jeopardy*, coiling it into a neat bundle and unfastening the end from around the stern cleat. "Let's go," she said. She stepped over the stern rail and onto the swim ladder. Then she stepped down into the dinghy.

I hesitated. If Patrick found out, he'd freak. I wondered if he could fail us for something like this. Olivia's face was pale in the moonlight, but she looked perfectly calm. "You sure you want to do this?"

She nodded impatiently. "If those men really are taking abalone, someone has to stop them."

"Okay." I stepped into the dinghy, sat down facing her and started rowing.

There was a slight current behind us—the tide coming in—and we were soon skimming along the water. It wasn't glassy calm like it had been that first evening, but it wasn't too bad: enough wind and waves to muffle the sound of our oars dipping into the water but not enough to make our lives difficult. Olivia was right—it was a perfect night for snooping. My nervousness started to fade. After all, it wasn't like we were really doing anything wrong.

As we approached the cabin cruiser, I stopped rowing and let the current carry us closer. Olivia held out one hand and, standing up carefully, grabbed onto the stern of the boat. I stood beside her. The cockpit was broad and open, quite different from a sailboat's. I strained my eyes staring at it but couldn't see much beyond the usual assortment of ropes and storage bags and at least a dozen empty beer bottles. If there were really only two guys onboard, they'd sure been putting it away.

I turned to Olivia. "Well?" I whispered. "Do you see anything?"

She looked disappointed. "When we rowed over before, I thought I saw shells on the deck. I mean, I know I did."

"Maybe you just..." I hesitated, not wanting to make her mad. "I mean, back in that restaurant in Port Hardy, you were talking about abalone and asking where it came from. Maybe, you know, because your dad's girlfriend did all that research on it—"

"You think I imagined it?" Olivia asked seriously. She didn't sound mad. "I guess it's possible, but honestly, I could have sworn those shells were abalone."

I shrugged. "Well, I can't see any shells now."

"No." She pointed at the open runabout fishing boat that was tied off the stern. "Let's just check in there. Maybe with the dive gear..."

We let go of the stern, and the dinghy started to drift backward toward the runabout. I pushed us away from the sharp propeller and steered us alongside. Olivia shone her flashlight into the boat, scanning from side to side. The dive gear wasn't there, nor were shells of any kind. The whole boat looked like it had been scrubbed clean.

"Well, I guess that's it," Olivia said flatly. "Maybe you were right, Simon."

I interrupted her. "Doesn't it seem kind of odd though?" I gestured to the runabout and then back to *Salty Mist*. "They've cleaned up everything. The dive gear, the shells you saw...why would they do that if they were just on holiday?"

"Maybe they just felt like cleaning," she said. "Not everyone's a slob, you know."

I ignored the implied insult. "Maybe."

We sat in silence for a moment. Olivia turned off her flashlight. "It is a bit of a coincidence," she said slowly. "Maybe when Patrick went over, they suspected something."

"He's not always the most subtle," I agreed. "If he asked too many questions, they might have got nervous."

"We have to get a closer look, don't we?" She looked at me. "There's only one way to do that."

I nodded. My hands were starting to sweat the way they always do when I get nervous. I knew exactly what she meant. We were going to have to get aboard that boat.

chapter twelve

As I tied the dinghy's towrope to *Salty Mist's* stern, I was grateful for the wind and the slight swell rolling into the anchorage. On a dead calm night, I wouldn't even have considered doing this. To be honest, the beer bottles made me feel a bit better too. If they'd drunk all of those tonight, it'd take more than a slight movement of the boat to wake them.

I remembered Olivia's cat feet and glanced down at my own runners. "We can't talk once we're aboard," I whispered. "Just signal to me if you hear anyone moving, okay? If anyone even stirs, we get the hell out of here and start rowing."

She nodded. Her eyes looked enormous.

Trying to move as slowly and quietly as possible, we stepped into *Salty Mist*'s cockpit and stood motionless for a moment, listening. Not a sound. Olivia held up her flashlight and raised her eyebrows questioningly. I shook my head. Not worth risking. Besides, between the full moon and the anchor light hanging over the cockpit, we could see pretty well.

Of course, that meant that anyone looking would see us pretty well too.

I hadn't been on a cabin cruiser before. It didn't have a small companionway with steps or a ladder leading down below like a sailboat; instead, it had full-height Plexiglas doors that opened directly into the cabin. I couldn't see inside—there were no lights on—but if the men woke and looked out, they'd see us right away. It was creepy, knowing that they could see us but we couldn't see them.

I gestured to Olivia that I was going forward. She nodded and indicated that she'd walk down the other side of the boat. Trying to walk as silently as possible, I crept toward the bow. Olivia was out of sight, on the other side of the cabin, and I had to fight a sudden irrational flood of fear that we shouldn't have separated. I couldn't see anything out of the ordinary, just some ropes hanging over the side of the boat and some water jugs strapped to a stainless-steel railing.

Something crunched under my foot. I froze, holding my breath. Nothing happened. Moving carefully, I bent down to pick up what I'd stepped on. A shell with an iridescent pearly sheen, now broken into three sharp-edged pieces. I slipped them in my pocket. Still crouching, I looked over my shoulder nervously. The cabin had large dark tinted windows all the way to the bow, and all it would take would be for one of the men to wake and glance out. Worst of all, the window right by me was open a few inches. I was only a few feet away from where the men were sleeping, without even a sheet of Plexiglas between us.

"Ssss." Olivia hissed softly, stepping out from behind the tall cabin and reappearing at the bow. She gestured to me to follow her.

I followed her across the wide flat deck at the front of the boat and back down her side of the cabin. "Look," I whispered, pulling out a piece of shell to show her.

She nodded and pulled a whole shell out of her own pocket.

I raised my eyebrows in a silent question and she nodded. "Abalone," she mouthed.

"Let's go then," I whispered. I figured we could show Patrick the shells. That'd convince him. We had to go back to Port Hardy anyway, and with a little luck, *Salty Mist* would still be sitting here when the authorities arrived.

Olivia held up her hand like she was telling me to wait a minute. Then she pointed to a rope hanging over the side of the boat. I shrugged and shook my head. I just wanted to get off this boat.

She started to pull up the rope, hand over hand.

"Careful," I whispered. Moving slowly, so as not to rock the boat, I bent close to see what she was doing. I don't know what I expected to see—just rope I guess, or maybe a fender—but what came up was a mesh bag, dripping wet. I leaned over the side and Olivia cupped her hand around her flashlight, pointed it at the bag and turned it on.

Abalone.

"Is it...are they alive?" I whispered.

She nodded. "They wouldn't be keeping them in the water if they weren't."

I glanced along the side of the boat. Rope after rope descended into the water. I remembered all the ropes that I'd seen hanging over the other side of the boat. More abalone, probably. A whole lot of abalone. "Let's go," I said. "Now."

Just then, a loud crackling voice shot out. Olivia grabbed my arm, and my heart just about stopped beating. We both froze, crouching low against the deck, right under that open window.

"Don't move," Olivia mouthed.

I shook my head. I couldn't have moved if I'd wanted to—my muscles seemed to have stopped working.

"*Salty Mist, Salty Mist*," the voice said, and I realized it was someone calling on the radio. The men would definitely be awake now, but maybe if we just stayed low and stayed still, we could sneak back to the dinghy after they went back to bed.

"Yo, *Salty Mist* here," someone on the boat responded. He sounded annoyed.

"Hi, it's *Jeopardy*. Switch to sixty-eight." Patrick's voice was tense.

Olivia shot me a startled look. There was a pause while the man changed his VHF to channel sixty-eight; then I heard Patrick's voice again.

"Hi, guys. Look, I've got a bit of a problem here...I woke up to take a leak and found a couple of my crew missing. They've taken the dinghy. Damn teenagers...Don't suppose you've seen them?"

My heart practically stopped. There was a click, and bright light suddenly spilled out the window. "Christ. What time is it?"

"Midnight. Look, I'm sorry I woke you but..."

I heard someone shuffling around inside the cabin and hoped like hell he wasn't going to come out here. If he saw the dinghy, we were screwed.

"Let me guess," the man said sleepily. "A girl and a guy, right?"

"Yeah." Patrick sounded worried, and I felt a flash of guilt.

The man laughed. "They're probably making out somewhere."

"They're the ones who rowed by your boat last night," Patrick said.

Right above our heads, the window slammed closed and we couldn't hear anymore. We stared at each other. "What now?" Olivia mouthed.

"We wait." My heart was beating so hard I could feel it in my whole body. I tried to breathe quietly. We kept looking at each other, eyes locked together, and for some stupid reason I noticed that Olivia was actually quite nice-looking under all that black hair.

Obviously, stress does odd things to the brain.

I heard the cabin door open, and I held my breath, waiting for the outraged shout of discovery when they saw the dinghy. But nothing happened. The door slid closed. After a minute, I started to breathe again. We must have left the towrope long enough that the dinghy had drifted back and been hidden by the runabout.

Finally, the light went off and all was still. I looked at Olivia. She held up five fingers. We waited—the longest, slowest, most agonizing five minutes of my life. Then we both crawled back to the cockpit, staying low enough that we wouldn't be seen in a casual glance out the tinted windows. As I untied the dinghy and tugged on the rope, I heard Olivia gasp.

Patrick was sitting in the dinghy, soaking wet and absolutely furious.

chapter thirteen

I jumped down into the dinghy.

Olivia crouched on *Salty Mist*'s stern. "Patrick, I'm so sorry," she whispered. "I'm really, really, really..."

"Did you swim over?" I asked, staring at him. "The water must be freezing."

His face was stiff with anger: his mouth a thin line, his eyes cold, his brows low. "Get in the dinghy, Olivia. What the hell are you two playing at?"

"Just listen," I said. "We can explain..."

"I woke up to take a leak, decided to go outside for a smoke and saw the dinghy gone." He pushed his wet hair off his face. "Thought one of you guys had tied a crappy knot and we'd lost it. Then...just in case...I checked your beds." He shook his head. "You have any idea how worried I was?"

"How'd you know where to find us?" Olivia asked.

Patrick stared at her like she was an idiot. "You've been like a broken record, going on about this boat. I figured it was worth checking. Swam halfway here, and then I spotted my dinghy."

"Look, we really are sorry," I said in a low voice. Please let me pass this course, I thought. I felt sick. If I failed...after all my saving and studying and planning...I couldn't even imagine telling my parents. I'd flunked enough at school, but sailing was supposed to be different.

"We didn't mean to worry you," I told him. "And we weren't just, you know, just goofing off. The thing is, we were pretty sure, well, Olivia was anyway, that those guys

95

were poaching." I fumbled in my pocket and pulled out the shell. "See? It's abalone."

He ignored me. "Get in the dinghy, Olivia."

Olivia didn't move. "They've got bags and bags of it hanging over the sides of the boat. Hundreds of abalone." Tears sparkled in her eyes. "It's so awful, Patrick. To do that... knowing a species is on the verge of extinction and to do that anyway, just to make a few bucks..."

"More than a few bucks," he said. "A lot more. On the shell, live abalone—well, they're probably getting forty or fifty dollars a pound." He shivered and wrapped his arms around himself. "Come on, Olivia, get in the damn dinghy. We should get out of here."

My mouth was open. Man, no kidding these guys didn't want anyone to know what they were doing. This was big business. Criminal, obviously, but big business nonetheless. I had to agree with Patrick—hanging around was not a good idea. "Yeah," I said, "let's get out of here."

She shook her head. "We should take the live abalone with us. Maybe it could still be saved."

Patrick's voice was low and urgent. "Olivia, these guys are making a small fortune off this. You don't want to mess with them."

Still squatting at the stern, Olivia struck her knees with her fists. "How can you put a price on the survival of a species?"

"It's not my price, honey. I'm just telling you what the market pays." He looked up at *Salty Mist*. "Mind you, they'll get a lower price for the meat they've already shucked and frozen."

"You think they've already...killed some of them?" she asked.

"I know they have. They've got a massive freezer." He sighed. "Here's how it works. They take their runabout out to dive for abalone to shuck and freeze. They spend a few days doing that—it's faster than trying to keep them alive, because they don't have to worry about damaging them."

"That's sick," Olivia breathed. She looked up at me. "Abalone are hemophiliacs, you know? If they're cut, they'll bleed to death."

"I didn't know," I said. I was feeling stunned, like things were moving too fast, like there was some important piece I hadn't quite figured out yet.

Patrick shrugged. "Then they spend a couple days diving and taking live abalone. The restaurants prefer it and it brings a higher price." He stood up and tried to grab Olivia's wrist, but she stepped backward. "Olivia, get in the goddamn dinghy," he hissed. "I'm not kidding around."

Olivia was staring at him. "Do you really know all this? Or are you just guessing? How do you know so much about it?"

I had a sudden flashback to sitting in that restaurant our first night in Port Hardy: Patrick's family's restaurant. Olivia spotting the abalone on the menu and Patrick saying, "Relax, it's imported."

"You buy it, don't you?" I said. "That abalone at your restaurant...it wasn't imported."

Olivia gasped. "Simon! That's an awful thing to say."

Patrick shrugged and his eyes slid away from us. "Lots of people buy it."

"How could you?" she said, raising her voice. "How could you do that?"

"Abalone sells," he said. "People don't ask where it comes from. And believe me, it's a whole lot cheaper to buy from Keith and Victor than to buy imported."

Above us on *Salty Mist* a light turned on, and the cabin door opened. A beam of light swept across the cockpit and landed on our dinghy. "I see you found your little runaways," a man's voice said. Then he laughed. "Did you swim over, Patrick? You'd better come aboard. I'll give you some dry clothes."

Patrick shook his head. "Thanks, Keith, but we'll just go. Sorry we disturbed you. Come on, Olivia."

Keith reached out and grabbed Olivia's arm. "I think you'd better all come aboard. I'd like to have a little talk with these two."

Olivia tried to pull her arm free, but the man held her tightly. "You're not going anywhere," he told her.

My heart was pounding. Patrick gave a resigned shrug, turning his hands up at his sides like there was nothing he could do now. He climbed up into *Salty Mist*'s cockpit and reached out a hand to me. I held back for a moment. I didn't want to go back onto that boat. Patrick and Olivia stood there, waiting for me. What else could I do? Jump overboard? Besides, I couldn't just abandon Olivia. I shrugged, and against all my instincts, I stepped aboard *Salty Mist*.

chapter fourteen

Olivia and I sat in the cockpit, side by side. My heart was racing and I felt shaky—anger, or nervousness, or both. Keith sat across from us, tugging on his short blond beard and not saying anything. He lit a cigarette and smoked, watching us.

"Go on in, Patrick," he said. "I'll keep an eye on your runaways." He raised his voice. "Victor! Get Patrick some dry clothes."

Patrick nodded and stepped inside, closing the door behind him. The lights in the cabin were dim compared with the deck light outside, and I couldn't see a thing through the dark Plexiglas doors. Keith stared at me, unsmiling. Beside me, Olivia's eyes were fixed on her running shoes. I hoped she wouldn't say anything that would make matters worse.

Inside the cabin, I could hear muffled voices, but I couldn't make out what they were saying. I wiped my sweaty palms against my pants. They were taking too long in there. And the longer they took, the more nervous I got. I'd figured that Patrick would get dressed, Olivia and I would get a lecture on minding our own business, and then we'd go back to *Jeopardy*. But now I was starting to think that maybe that wasn't what was going to happen at all. I looked at Olivia and wished we could talk for a minute, privately.

I started to do some math, which was something I usually avoided. It didn't make me feel any better. If Victor and Keith were really selling the abalone at forty or fifty dollars a pound, we were talking about some serious money. They were not going to be happy if Patrick told them what we had discovered. I looked at Keith, sitting silently across the cockpit in a white T-shirt and track pants, and I couldn't help noticing the thick muscles bunching in his shoulders and neck. I swallowed nervously. He didn't look like the kind of guy you wanted mad at you.

Finally the door opened, and Patrick came out with Victor right behind him.

Victor was tall and skinny, middle-aged, with fair hair buzzed short behind a receding hairline. He wasn't as obviously muscular as Keith, but there was something about his face—a hardness around his thin mouth, a deadness in his small deep-set eyes—that made me shiver. "Well, it looks like we've got a bit of a problem here," he said softly. He shook his head and looked from me to Olivia and then back to me again.

"Look, it's no problem," I said, thinking quickly. "We're sorry we disturbed you and all that. We just wanted to get off our boat and explore a little, you know?" I nudged Olivia, hoping she'd clue in. "We don't really care what you guys are doing. It's none of our business."

"Since when are you two minding your own business?" Patrick asked. He sounded resigned. "I think we all know you came over here to snoop."

Shut up, Patrick, shut up. I tried to think fast, to make up some story about what we were doing, but I didn't know how much Patrick had already told them. He looked just like he always did—the crooked smile, the blue eyes, the easy relaxed posture. But he was standing over us, and beside him Victor was clenching and unclenching his fists.

I backtracked and spoke directly to Victor and Keith. "Okay, I admit that. We were curious about your boat and what you were diving for. Like I said, I'm sorry. We had no right to be snooping around, and we'll stay away now."

"Bit late for that," Victor said. His voice was a harsh whisper. He looked at Keith. "Patrick says they saw the abalone."

My heart was banging away like crazy, and my hands were cold and sweaty. Victor looked like the kind of guy who might decide that smacking us around a bit might teach us a lesson. I tried to look relaxed, which took some pretty impressive acting. I leaned back and opened my arms wide. "Look, guys, I'm really sorry. But like I said, it's none of our business what you're doing here."

Olivia looked at me like I was nuts. "It's absolutely our business. It's everyone's business." She looked at Victor and at Keith. "Abalone is a threatened species. The reason you're not allowed to catch it is because the numbers have declined dramatically since people started diving for them and harvesting them to sell." She leaned toward them, eyes wide. "There is a real chance of northern abalone becoming an endangered species. Surely you don't want to contribute to that?"

I closed my eyes, groaning inwardly. She sounded as passionate as a TV evangelist trying to persuade her audience to see the light. Only this audience wasn't likely to be converted.

Victor started to laugh, and my eyes flew open again at the sound. It was the creepiest laugh I'd ever heard: soft, harsh and utterly chilling. Even under the bright deck light, his pupils were huge, and I wondered if he was on drugs. "You're going to report us as soon as you get back to Hardy, aren't you?" he said.

I jabbed my elbow into Olivia's ribs and hoped she'd take the hint. "Of course not," I said. "It's none of our business."

"Right. That's why you were snooping around our boat."

I shrugged, feeling helpless. "We won't report you."

"Do you know what would happen if we got caught?" he asked.

I shook my head, trying to remember what Patrick had said. "Not really. A fine, right?"

Keith answered, "A huge fine, on top of the money we'd be losing by not selling what we've got onboard. We've got a full freezer of shucked meat, plus a couple hundred pounds of live abalone, and we've got buyers waiting for all of it." He grinned. "Got a wholesale seafood company in Vancouver that'll take as much frozen abalone as we can get."

"But that's the least of it," Victor cut in. "We could get jail time. For sure, they'd con-fiscate our boats and our dive gear. That's a couple hundred thousand bucks right there."

I swallowed hard. I'd had no idea the stakes were so high. No wonder Patrick had tried to keep us away. "I promise," I said. "I give you my word we won't tell." Olivia, please don't say anything, I thought. She was a smart girl, but her timing sure sucked sometimes.

"Your word," Victor said, laughing. "What do you think, Patrick? Can we trust his word?"

Patrick shifted from one foot to the other. His blue eyes met mine for a second and then flickered away. My heart sank. If Patrick wasn't going to stick up for us, we were screwed.

"I don't know," he said at last. "But even if they do report this, they've got no proof. You could dump the abalone and be long gone by the time anyone showed up."

"Ah, but then they'd be watching us like hawks," Victor said, shaking his head. "We couldn't make a move without the Fisheries guys being all over us. If your pals here make a report, they'll be putting us right out of the abalone business."

Keith stood up, his broad shoulders and thick neck suddenly looking even more intimidating. The guy probably weighed more than Olivia and me put together. "Can't risk it," he said.

Olivia's leg was pressed against mine, and I could feel it shaking. Or maybe it was me that was shaking. I had a terrible feeling that I knew where this conversation was headed, but I still couldn't quite believe it. Stuff like this only happened in the movies. Didn't it?

chapter fifteen

I looked around the cockpit for anything we could use to defend ourselves. On a sailboat, there might have been a heavy winch handle, or even a knife strapped to the compass post. But I couldn't see anything but a bucket and a few coiled ropes. I glanced back at the three men. Short of having a gun in my hand, I couldn't even imagine fighting them. I mean, I'm five-foot-six, 120 pounds, and unfortunately I've never done any martial arts in my life. I snuck a peek at Olivia, who was even smaller than me. It sure would be nice if she turned out to have a black belt in Karate, but I figured her to be more of the ballet- and piano-lessons type.

I glanced around again. No guns. Well, on the bright side at least we weren't about to get shot. Then I saw something. Just a couple of feet to my right, beside the cabin door, was a VHF radio. A small handheld, just lying there, tucked in the corner where someone had forgotten to put it away. If I could just grab it... but there was no way. I'd have to pick it up, turn it on, turn to channel sixteen and then explain our location and situation. All with three, large, angry men within a few feet of me. Nope. Wasn't going to happen.

Besides, odds were that no one was within range anyway.

Except *Jeopardy*. And that gave me an idea. Maybe if we yelled, maybe if we made a whole lot of noise, Blair and Joey would hear us.

I stood up and yelled as loudly as I could. "Help! Help! We're on—" An enormous hand whacked me across the face, knocking my glasses off, smashing into my nose and mashing my lip against my teeth. Pain exploded in a flash of red and black, driving all thoughts from my mind for a few seconds.

"Don't do that again," Victor advised me. His voice was flat and cold, but his lips were curled in a tooth-baring snarl.

Olivia started to cry. "This is all my fault," she said. "I was the one who wanted to come over here. Simon didn't care what you guys are doing. Please just let him go. He won't tell anyone about the abalone."

My mouth was full of blood and I ran my tongue along my teeth, checking to make sure they were all still there. A couple of hundred feet away *Jeopardy* sat still and silent in the water. No lights turned on. I braced myself and yelled again. "Joey! Blair!"

Victor grabbed me and shoved me back down on the bench, pressing one hand against my mouth. "Duct tape," he said, like a surgeon asking for a scalpel. Keith opened a cockpit locker, pulled out a monster-sized roll and started wrapping it around my head, covering my mouth completely.

I felt like I was suffocating. Can't breathe, I tried to say, but I couldn't open my lips, and all that came out was a strangled grunt. Frantic for air, I tried to grab the duct tape and tear it away from my mouth. Keith caught my wrists in his massive hands. He pulled them behind my back roughly and started duct-taping them together. My heart was hammering in my chest, and I desperately needed to open my mouth and gasp for breath. This is it, I thought. I'm going to die.

They were going to kill us. It sounded crazy, but I was pretty sure I was right. Our lives were worth less to them than the abalone.

Then I had an idea. A crazy idea—an idea that probably wasn't going to work—but I didn't have anything to lose. I let myself be shoved back down to the bench, pretending to lose my balance so that I landed a couple of feet away from Olivia. Closer to the cabin doors. Almost on top of that VHF radio.

"So, do we need to tape you up like your friend, or can you keep your mouth shut?" Keith asked Olivia.

"I'll be quiet," she whispered.

Patrick looked at me, and his forehead creased in concern. "Um, I think Simon's having some trouble breathing."

"Doesn't much matter," Victor said. "He's not going to be breathing for much longer anyway."

Olivia choked back a sob. I wished I could tell her what I was going to do, but perhaps it was better not to get her hopes up. There was a lot of blood all down my shirt, and I wondered if my nose was broken. I was frantic for air, and for a moment a rising tide of panic almost overwhelmed me.

Stay calm, I told myself. Stay calm. I concentrated on keeping my breathing slow and even. Then, trying not to let any other part of my body move, I fumbled behind my back with my bound hands. Where was that VHF? I felt around frantically.

Got it. And there was the Transmit button on the side. I couldn't say anything, but maybe...just maybe...I wouldn't have to.

I had to turn it on without changing the channel. Odds were good that it had been left turned to 16—the hailing and distress channel, the channel most boats monitored...and most importantly, the channel that *Jeopardy*'s radio was set to. I could feel three small knobs. One had to be the on-off-volume switch. Most likely, I thought, the first one, the one on the left. I hesitated for a second. If I turned the wrong knob—turned the radio away from channel 16—no one would hear us. And if the main radio in the cabin was still turned on, they'd all hear their conversation being broadcast, and they'd know what I was up to right away. And if my finger slipped off the Transmit button, even for a second, Keith, Victor and Patrick would hear the static of the radio, and that would be the end.

No one was looking at me. Keith nodded at the other two men. "Victor's right. If they don't make it back to Port Hardy, they won't be reporting anything." He looked at Patrick. "How about if you just go back to your boat? Swim back. In the morning, you can discover the dinghy gone and two of your students missing."

Nothing to lose, I reminded myself. My hands were clumsy and my fingers turning numb from the tightness of the duct tape, but I managed to wedge the VHF against the back of the bench. Then, holding down the Transmit button with one finger, I twisted the first knob clockwise.

Then all I could do was hope.

chapter sixteen

"So, I leave and you guys deal with these two. And then what?" Patrick asked, frowning. "I call the Coast Guard in the morning? Report them missing? Organize a search?"

"Yeah. But it'll be too late," Victor said. "They'll stay missing. And we'll be long gone."

Olivia stared at Patrick. "This isn't really happening. You wouldn't let them kill us."

Patrick couldn't meet her eyes. "Look," he said. He hesitated, clearing his throat. "Look, you guys got yourselves into this situation. I did my best to keep you away, didn't I? I warned you not to interfere."

I tried to catch Olivia's eyes. She looked at me, her eyes shiny with tears. "I'm sorry," she whispered.

I shook my head, trying to tell her it wasn't her fault. Play for time, I thought, wishing she could read my mind. Keep them talking.

She seemed to have the same idea. "Patrick...you don't really want to do this, do you? I mean, you're not a killer."

"Patrick is a lot smarter than you. He knows when to butt out." Victor laughed. "Besides, we keep him supplied with more than abalone."

Drugs, I thought. I'd been right about Victor being high. I'd bet if we had a chance to look around the boat a bit more, we'd find some bags of white powder hidden away. If these guys were dealing drugs too, they had one more reason to avoid being caught.

I desperately needed to breathe. I was starting to feel dizzy and sitting here, half-suffocating, was unbearable. I tried not to move but I couldn't help it. I jerked forward, and my hands slipped off the VHF.

There was a loud burst of static, and everyone froze for a second. Keith lunged forward and threw me off the bench onto the cockpit floor. I lay there, unable to move, unable to breathe, staring up at Olivia and hoping she could tell somehow that I was in real trouble.

"What the hell?" Keith hissed. "Did you turn this on? Because it's not gonna do you much good with your mouth taped shut."

"Tie up the girl," Victor said. "We can just dump them both overboard."

Keith pulled Olivia to her feet, yanked her arms behind her back and wrapped them with duct tape. This is it, I thought hopelessly. We were both going to be killed, and there was nothing I could do about it. I was as helpless as the damn abalone.

"You can't dump them here," Patrick pointed out. "There'll be a search, and if they find them tied up..."

I couldn't believe he was talking about it so calmly.

"He's right," Keith said. "It'd be better if it looked like they died of natural causes." His face lit up. "Or an overdose."

Victor nodded, a satisfied smirk curling his lips. "That's perfect. Everyone will think they just snuck away from the sailboat to get high." He headed into the cabin.

Keith followed him, turning to talk to Patrick over his shoulder. "Keep an eye on them. We'll just get the stuff."

My mouth was full of blood and I kept swallowing, terrified that I was going to choke. I wondered if my parents would believe that I'd overdosed. They knew I didn't use drugs. But maybe they'd just figure I hadn't been honest with them. It wasn't like we were all that close. I wished I had a chance to tell them...to tell them...Everything was starting to go black.

"Look," Patrick said, "I'm sorry about this. I mean, I never wanted you guys to get hurt but..."

Then I heard another voice. "Get in the cabin," it said. I twisted my head around and struggled to see. Without my glasses, everything was a blur, but I could see Patrick standing by the cabin door. "He's got a gun," he yelled and dove into the cabin.

I heard the cabin door slamming shut behind him. A gun? Who? Nothing made sense. Then cold water was dripping all over me, and someone was ripping the duct tape off my mouth. I took a loud heaving gulp of air, and another and another. My chest hurt, but it was the best feeling ever.

"Come on, man," Joey said. "Get up." He was standing over me, soaking wet. I'd never in my life been so glad to see anyone.

"What...what...," I gasped, trying to stand, my hands still behind my back. I looked around. Blair was standing warily by the cabin door, a gun in his hand. A bright, orange gun. I blinked a couple of times and realized what it was: the flare gun from *Jeopardy*. Joey handed him a loose padlock from one of the cockpit lockers, and Blair used it to lock the door. On the other side, behind the dark Plexiglas, I could hear the three men shouting and swearing.

"Jeez..." I tried to think, but nothing quite made sense. I stepped toward Olivia, grinning. "I'll untie you," I said. "Umm..." I realized my own hands were still tied.

"My hero," Olivia said sarcastically.

Joey noticed our predicament and came to the rescue, unwrapping the tight layers of sticky duct tape and freeing first my hands and then Olivia's. I fumbled on the floor, found my glasses and put them on. Everything slid back into focus.

"What if they manage to climb out a window?" Olivia whispered. "I bet the tall skinny guy could fit."

Blair shrugged. "Then I guess I'll shoot them."

"Would that work?" I asked quietly. "I mean, it's just a flare gun."

We all looked at each other. None of us knew the answer. Patrick had yelled, "He's got a gun!" He would have recognized his own flare gun though. Had he been trying to save us somehow, to give us a chance to get away?

"Let's get out of here," Olivia said.

121

"We'd better take their runabout," I said. "It'll be faster than the sailboat."

Olivia nodded agreement. "I'll see if the keys are in it."

A minute later, she was back, shaking her head. "We'll have to take *Jeopardy*."

"Then we better do something about this boat," I said. My brain finally seemed to be working again. "Once we're gone— once Blair's not standing there with a gun in his hand—they'll manage to squeeze out a window, or at least the skinny guy will, and he'll let the others out. We need to make sure they can't follow us."

"Well, let's hope there's engine access from out here," Olivia said. "I don't really feel like going inside."

We all followed her gaze to the cabin door. "No kidding," I said.

Olivia dropped to her knees and lifted a panel by her feet. "There it is," she said softly.

I looked down at the engine: a big gray mass of metal and hoses and belts. Unfortunately, I've never been very interested in engines.

"Does anyone know anything about diesels?" I asked.

"I do," Olivia said.

The men were pounding on the door and yelling. Ignoring them, Olivia bent down. "That's the fuel line. If we cut that, they won't get any gas to their engine. I need something sharp."

Joey opened a cockpit locker and rummaged around. He lifted out a toolbox and plonked it down on the floor beside Olivia.

She pulled out a utility knife and began slashing away methodically. Finally, she looked up at us. "Fuel line cut, water intake hose cut, electrical wires cut. *Salty Mist* isn't going anywhere."

"Nice work," I told her, nodding. I was impressed.

She grinned; then she leaned over and tapped her finger against the fuel gauge. "Their gas tank's pretty low. Let's take the extra jerry cans, just in case," she said.

It seemed like overkill to me, but I grabbed the fuel jugs that were strapped to the stern rail and lowered them into our dinghy. "What about the runabout? Should we take it with us?"

She hesitated. "Isn't that stealing?"

Joey snorted. "These guys were going to kill you, Olivia. I think we can justify taking their boat."

"Just untie it," Blair said. "It'll drift away pretty fast. Towing it will slow *Jeopardy* down."

Joey untied the runabout, and we watched the current carry it away from us.

"Ready to go?" Blair asked, still pointing the flare gun warily in the direction of the cabin.

I looked down at the mess Olivia had made of the engine. "Yeah," I said. "Let's get out of here."

chapter seventeen

I started the dinghy's outboard engine, and we flew across the anchorage, pounding into the small waves and sending sheets of spray into the air.

Olivia let out a long sigh. "Thank you guys so much. I thought we were dead." Then she frowned. "But how did you know? Did you hear Simon yell?"

Blair shook his head. "No." Then he frowned. "Well, maybe that was what woke me. I don't know. I heard Patrick talking to someone on the radio in the middle of the night, but I was pretty tired so I didn't really pay attention. It was odd though."

"I heard that too," Joey said. "But I went back to sleep, and then something else woke me. I got up to pee, and I noticed that Olivia was gone. Then we heard her voice on the radio."

Olivia looked puzzled. "My voice?"

"Yeah. You said something about Patrick letting some guys kill you. And then I heard those men talking and—"

"But how were we on the radio?" Olivia asked. Then she got it. She turned to me, laughing. "You pushed Transmit on that radio, didn't you? You couldn't talk, so you just let Blair and Joey hear the whole thing. That's...brilliant."

I grinned modestly. "Well..."

"Course, getting your nose broken wasn't so smart," she said.

Gingerly touching my swollen nose, I had to agree. "Thought I was going to drown in my own blood when they taped my mouth," I said. I couldn't help shuddering as I remembered how scared I'd been and how close we'd come to dying.

"Yeah. You weren't looking too good when we arrived." Joey shot me a sympathetic smile. "Your glasses are totally crooked, you know."

We were drawing close to *Jeopardy*, its glossy hull gleaming against the darkness of the water. Above it, the moon shone silvery-bright and a million stars lit the sky. I tried to straighten my glasses, but they were bent out of shape from getting hit. There was a lump in my throat all of a sudden, and I swallowed hard. "If you guys hadn't come... well. Thanks a lot. I mean, you could've been killed too. And bringing the flare gun...that was smart."

"Saw it in a movie," Blair said. "Anyway, it's no big thing. You guys helped us out earlier. Olivia, you know, with making a sling for my arm; and you helped out Joey after the knock down."

I looked at him incredulously. "It's hardly the same."

Blair shrugged. "It's cool, man. We're a team."

My eyes were suddenly wet and I turned away, not wanting anyone to see. The thing was, since I first met them, I'd kind of dismissed Joey and Blair as the rich, take-everything-for-granted type. I'd done just what my dad always does—assumed, because of the way they looked, that they were spoiled lazy snobs. But they'd just risked their lives to save mine and they wouldn't even let me thank them for it.

"How's your arm?" I asked, feeling awkward.

"It's fine." He rubbed his wrist experimentally. "Just bruised. How's your nose?"

"All right." Actually, it hurt, a lot, but at least it had finally stopped bleeding.

"You look like you got stabbed or something," Olivia said. "You're covered in blood." She grinned at me. "Not a good look."

I grinned back at her. "No doubt." We bumped alongside *Jeopardy*'s hull. I cut the engine, and we all scrambled aboard. Everything looked the same, safe and familiar, but I had to remind myself that the night wasn't over yet. A couple of hundred feet away were three men who wanted us dead. I stared across the dark anchorage to where *Salty Mist*'s deck light still shone brightly. No sign of movement yet, but it wouldn't be long before they managed to get out. I didn't want to be sitting here when they did. "We better haul the anchor and get out of here," I said reluctantly.

Blair nodded, but Olivia looked anxious. "In the dark? Can't we call for help or something?"

Joey shook his head. "Patrick said we were out of range, remember?" He suddenly grinned. "But maybe not for my cell phone though."

He disappeared into the cabin. We all waited, our eyes on *Salty Mist*.

"We don't have to go far, but if we stay here, there's nothing to stop them swimming over and taking another shot at killing us," I pointed out. "So let's go."

Olivia nodded and hastily jumped down the companionway steps to open the engine intake. I sprinted to the bow and began hauling up the anchor. Blair started the engine and pulled out the chart and the GPS.

"We can't see much, so we'll have to be really careful," he said. "I'll program in some waypoints to take us out of the harbor and back into the channel. We can head back toward Port Hardy." He looked at his watch. "It's almost three thirty. It'll start getting light in a couple of hours."

Finally the anchor was up, clunking back on its steel roller. "Let's go," I yelled.

Joey climbed back into the cockpit, and we all looked at him hopefully. "Any luck?" I asked.

He shook his head. "Sorry, guys. My phone was sitting in a puddle of salt water. It's not working at all."

It looked like we were on our own. Olivia turned *Jeopardy* in the direction of the harbor entrance and we were off. We all turned to take a final look at *Salty Mist*. Over the noise of our engine, I heard a shout. Victor must have made it out the window. We'd taken the padlock key, but they probably had a spare key inside the cabin. If Victor was free, the others soon would be too. Olivia looked at me for a second, eyes wide and scared. Then she pushed the throttle forward. Picking up speed, *Jeopardy* cut through the water, leaving *Salty Mist* and Victor's angry shouts behind us.

I sat down in the cockpit, suddenly exhausted. We were all silent, listening to the hum of *Jeopardy*'s engine and the sounds of the wind and the water. It felt odd to be out here, just the four of us, sailing into the darkness.

"Umm, Simon? Should we raise the mainsail?" Joey asked uncertainly.

I looked up at the broken spreader. "I don't know," I said slowly. "Maybe we shouldn't risk it." The wind was blowing fairly hard, and the thought of the sail filling with wind and straining against the rigging made me nervous.

"Yeah," Blair agreed. "Let's just motor."

Soon we were out in the channel, Vancouver Island on our starboard side and Hope Island on our port. Not that we could see much—just dark outlines against a dark sky. "Blair, did you get those waypoints programmed into the GPS? What heading should we be on?"

"Actually, this is good as we are. Just stay on this course. It's twenty-four miles to Port Hardy," Blair said. He was holding a small flashlight between his teeth as he measured off the distance on the chart.

I looked down at the knotmeter. Five knots. "Five hours," I said. "If all goes well."

And then, without warning, the engine spluttered and died. We were drifting silently into the darkness.

chapter eighteen

Engine failure. I couldn't believe it. I mean, we'd just managed to get away from three men who were prepared to kill us, and I figured we deserved a bit of a break. It didn't look like we were going to get one.

To my surprise, everyone seemed to be looking to me for direction. I shrugged and turned to Olivia. "Well, you're the mechanic. Any ideas?"

She wrinkled her forehead and started muttering something about the color of the exhaust and water in the fuel. Then she disappeared down below to stare at the engine.

I looked at Joey and Blair. "I think we're going to have to raise the sails," I told them. "At least the wind is coming over our starboard side, so the strain won't be on the broken spreader."

They both nodded. "Right. But if we have to tack..." Blair frowned.

"Yeah. Then I guess we'll find out whether that halyard is strong enough to support the mast." We all looked up. The thought of a forty-foot-high metal pole crashing down onto the deck was not comforting.

"Maybe Olivia will have fixed the engine by then," Joey said optimistically. "I'll go help her."

Blair was still holding his injured wrist close to his side, so I suggested that he take the helm while I raised the sails. Then I scrambled up to the mast. There was a decent breeze, and I figured we wanted to make some time, so I opted for a full main and working jib. I shackled the main halyard to the top of the sail, removed the sail ties and looked toward Blair. "Ready?"

He loosened the main sheet and nodded. "Yeah. Raise the mainsail!"

I wrapped the halyard around the winch and began pulling hand over hand, raising the sail. *Jeopardy* had turned itself bow into the wind, so the sail began to luff, flapping noisily from side to side. Blair turned the steering wheel to bear off, turning the bow of the boat away from the wind. The sail filled with wind, and immediately *Jeopardy* heeled over slightly and began to move forward through the water. I grinned to myself. That moment when the engine is silent and the sails fill and lift the boat through the water... well, it's magic. Despite everything, it felt good to be sailing. I looked back at Blair and whooped loudly.

"Spacey, you're one crazy kid," Blair said. He was grinning back at me though.

"Shall I raise the jib?"

"Go for it."

Still smiling, I made my way up to the fore-deck. Holding onto the forestay for balance,

I clipped the jib halyard onto the foresail; then I undid the ties that were holding the sail in a tight bundle on the deck. We should be wearing our safety harnesses, I thought. If someone went overboard in the dark, it'd be impossible to spot them. The thought reminded me of something and I laughed. "Hey, Blair?" I shouted.

"Yeah?"

"Remember when I thought Joey had gone overboard?"

"Yeah." He started to laugh. "That was pretty funny."

"I didn't think so at the time, but it was, wasn't it?" I pictured Joey popping up from down below and telling us he'd just been taking a dump, and I started cracking up. "I guess I must have looked pretty stunned when he appeared, huh?"

"You did." Blair's shoulders were shaking with laughter. "Sorry we called you Spacey and all that though."

"You still call me Spacey."

He stopped laughing and looked thoughtful. "Yeah, but...it's different now."

I raised the jib; then I sprinted back to the cockpit to tighten the jib sheet as the wind pushed the sail over to the port side. *Jeopardy* picked up speed, humming through the darkness. Blair and I were both grinning like idiots. I felt like I should say something: thanks for saving my life, maybe, or sorry I misjudged you. But then our eyes met, and he nodded, and I thought maybe nothing really needed to be said after all.

Olivia popped her head up from down below. "Umm, guys?"

"Yeah?"

"We don't have a clue what's wrong with the engine."

I shrugged. "It's a sailboat. Who needs an engine?"

Olivia flashed me a smile as bright as white sails in sunlight, climbed into the cockpit and sat down beside me. I had an urge to put my arm around her shoulder, just because I was so glad we were both still alive, but I had the sense not to. I doubted she'd appreciate it. So I just sat there, a goofy grin spreading across my face as we sailed into the velvety darkness.

It was dream sailing: calm water, a decent breeze, the wind off the beam—despite the darkness, it was about as comfortable a sail as you could ask for. Everything that had happened now seemed completely unreal. Of course, when we arrived in Port Hardy, we'd have a lot to explain...but for now, it was just the four of us, on a fabulous boat, sailing through the night.

We watched as the sky slowly brightened along the eastern horizon. The sky was a clear cloudless indigo and a lighter streak formed a sharp pale band, slowly widening. It was going to be a beautiful day.

Joey yawned widely. "Breakfast, don't you think?" He disappeared into the cabin and re-emerged a couple of minutes later with a tray of food: a tin of cashews, some oranges, a loaf of bread, a jar of peanut butter, some chocolate bars and a bag of sour-cream-and-onion chips.

Olivia took a Snickers bar and peeled back its wrapper. "Not exactly classic breakfast food, but I'm not complaining. In fact, I think this might be the first meat-free meal of our trip."

I surveyed the spread and sighed. "I could've gone for a steak. A nice, rare, bloody one." Olivia wrinkled her nose in disgust, and I laughed. I didn't think I'd ever been so hungry in my life. I could barely shovel the food in fast enough. We all sat in contented silence, just the sounds of the wind and the sea, and the occasional belch from Joey.

Then I heard something else: a sound that sent a sudden flood of cold rushing through my body. An engine, thrumming in the distance. I stood up and turned around. "I hate to say this...but I think I can hear another boat coming."

Blair and Olivia stood quickly, and we all scanned the channel behind us. A long way behind us, a small white shape was rapidly getting larger.

chapter nineteen

We all stood in the cockpit, staring over the stern. The boat was gaining on us fast.

"Olivia...could they have fixed the engine? After everything you did to it?" I held my breath.

She frowned and twisted her mouth to one side. "If they had enough spare hose and electrical wire...sure."

"It might not be them," Joey said.

I nodded. "It might not."

We were all quiet for a moment.

I looked at the knotmeter. Five knots. Then I studied the sails. "We can go faster than this," I said. I let out the main sheet slightly and pulled the jib in tighter, distracting myself by fine-tuning and adjusting the sails and watching the boat respond, picking up speed. I imagined myself racing *Jeopardy* back home, imagined myself captain of a beautiful boat flying across the—

"Six and a half knots." Blair looked up. "But Simon..."

"I know." I couldn't afford to space out now. The other boat was closer, close enough to see that it was a cabin cruiser, white with blue canvas. I didn't need to be able to read the name on the hull to know it was *Salty Mist*. No amount of trimming the sails would help: A sailboat can't outrace a powerboat.

Everyone was looking at me, and I didn't know what to do. This sort of thing hadn't been covered in any of our reading or lessons on how to handle emergencies at sea. Emergencies...Emergencies...Something clicked. "Call a Mayday," I said.

Olivia looked at me. "Simon, we're out of range, remember? We already talked about it." She had that look on her face that meant she was thinking Spacey but not saying it.

"But it was Patrick who said we were out of range. And obviously he'd say that. You wanted to report abalone poaching." I was talking fast, my words spilling out. I jumped down into the cabin, switched on the radio, and bringing the mike with me, climbed back into the cockpit.

She was nodding. "Of course. Besides, even if he was actually telling the truth, we're way closer to Port Hardy now."

I pushed the Transmit button and, with a shiver, remembered the last time I'd done that. Then I hesitated. "Should I call Mayday? Or just, you know...ask for help?"

"Mayday calls are for clear and imminent danger," Olivia said, quoting from our manual. "I'd say this qualifies."

I couldn't really argue with that. "Mayday, Mayday, Mayday," I said clearly. "This is the sailing vessel *Jeopardy*. We are—" I broke off. "Where are we?"

Blair looked at the chart. "Just about eight miles north of Port Hardy, I think."

"Eight miles north of Port Hardy," I repeated, hoping he was right. I hadn't been paying too much attention to the navigation. "In the Goletas Channel. We're in need of assistance."

Olivia looked at me, eyebrows disappearing under her hair. "In need of assistance? That sounds like we're just running out of gas or something."

"Well, what do you want me to say? That some men are trying to kill us?" I snuck a peek over my shoulder. *Salty Mist* was closing the gap fast.

"Yes!"

There was a loud explosion in my ears and my heart stopped beating for a moment. I looked around, my ears still ringing. Joey was standing at the stern rail, the flare gun in his hand, and a red plume of smoke was snaking high into the sky.

"Give us some warning next time," I said, pressing my hand over my jack-hammering heart. Then I spoke into the radio again.

"We're setting off flares. We are being chased by a cabin cruiser called *Salty Mist* and the men onboard just tried to kill us. Umm, over."

We all waited. I hoped Patrick had lied about us being out of range. I hoped that someone was out there, listening, and that they wouldn't dismiss our call as a prank. I hoped we hadn't escaped just to be caught again.

And then a voice responded. *"Jeopardy*, this is the Coast Guard. Please repeat your location and the nature of your distress. Over."

Olivia, Blair and Joey all started whooping with relief and excitement, and I had to shush them before I responded. "We're in the Goletas Channel about eight miles northwest of Port Hardy..." I trailed off, reluctant to say it. I glanced over my shoulder and saw *Salty Mist*, only a few hundred feet away. "Well, the men on this other boat kind of tried to kill us, and now they're chasing after us, and they're really close. Umm, over."

"Roger." The operator sounded completely calm, her voice flat and nasal. I wondered if she'd actually understood what I'd just said.

"*Jeopardy*, switch to channel 83."

I changed to 83 quickly, fighting panic. *Salty Mist* was getting awfully close. "Coast Guard, this is *Jeopardy*."

In the same calm, flat voice, the radio operator asked for the details of our situation. Standing at the stern, Blair was signalling me to hurry up. "We were...these men were poaching abalone...Umm..." *Salty Mist* was so close now that I could see Victor standing at the bow. I couldn't think. I took my finger off the Transmit button. "Olivia? Can you explain? I'll..." I trailed off. I didn't know what I was going to do, but I had to do something.

Olivia nodded, took the microphone and in a voice almost as calm as the operator's, she started to explain what had happened.

At the helm, Blair was holding us on course, his face grim. Joey was standing at the stern, loading another flare into the flare gun. "Any ideas?" I asked them.

"I was thinking about shooting a flare at their boat," Joey said. "If it made a hole in the hull, maybe they'd sink."

"Try it," I said. "Nothing to lose."

Salty Mist was almost on top of us now, coming up on our starboard side and slowing down to match our pace. Keith was at the wheel, up top on the fly bridge. I couldn't see Patrick and wondered where he was. Joey fired the flare gun, and we all clapped our hands over our ears.

A plume of red smoke hung in the air, but *Salty Mist* didn't slow down.

"Just bounced off her hull," Joey muttered in disgust. "Useless."

"They're trying to get alongside," I said. I watched Victor, standing at the bow, his eyes fixed on *Jeopardy*. "I bet Victor's going to try to jump across to our boat."

"Well, let's make it harder for them," Blair said. "Let's turn around or something."

"We'll have to jibe," I said. The easiest way to turn a sailboat is to tack—to turn the bow of the boat through the wind—but with *Salty Mist* so close on our windward side, that wasn't an option. Jibing means turning the boat away from the wind, so that the stern of the boat moves through the wind instead of the bow. It's more difficult, but I'd done it plenty of times. I just hadn't done it on a boat with broken rigging.

chapter twenty

Salty Mist eased a little closer, and Victor was poised to jump. "Let's do it," I yelled. Blair turned the wheel to port, and *Jeopardy* responded, turning away from *Salty Mist*. I held my breath. I had to wait until the wind was almost behind us—if I pulled the main sheet in tight too soon, we'd lose speed and possibly steerage, which would be a disaster in this situation. But if I waited too long, the wind could catch the boom and send it crashing across the cockpit. I wasn't sure how much strain our broken rigging could handle.

Now. I pulled the main sheet in tight, bringing the boom across the center of the boat. "Ready!"

Blair turned the wheel further to port. "Jibe ho!" he yelled as the wind pushed the boom across the center line. I quickly eased the main sheet and the sail filled with wind. Joey released the jib and let the wind push it over; then he hauled the sheets in. We were off. I looked up at the rigging. Everything seemed to be holding together just fine.

"Nice," Blair said, grinning at me.

Of course, powerboats like *Salty Mist* can turn on a dime, without having to worry about wind direction or sails. Within thirty seconds, it was pulling alongside again. "Now what?" Blair asked.

"Do it again," I said grimly. "The more we move, the harder we'll be to catch."

Blair nodded, and we repeated our maneuver, jibing again. Not quite as smoothly this time, but everything held together.

Olivia appeared beside us. "They're sending a boat, with police officers." She stared at *Salty Mist*, which was once again trying to ease close alongside. "But it might take them half an hour to get here."

"They're idiots if they try to do anything to us now," Blair said, nodding at *Salty Mist*. "I mean, the cops know who they are, you've told them everything. They won't get away with it."

"Yeah. But they don't seem to be giving up, do they?" I said. I stood on the bench and yelled as loud as I could, "The cops are on their way! Give it up!"

Victor made a rude gesture, and *Salty Mist* veered so close that for a moment, I thought we might collide.

"Again," I said. "Now."

Jeopardy jibed neatly, and we were heading downwind, back on a port tack. As before, *Salty Mist* spun around and moved in again. When I looked up, Olivia's eyes were shiny wet.

"Don't worry," I said awkwardly. I wanted to reassure her that we'd be okay but I wasn't sure I believed it myself. "We'll figure out something."

She shook her head. "It's the abalone," she said. "All the live abalone hanging over the side of their boat. I'd hoped it could still be returned to the water, but if they've been dragging it along, I bet it's all dead."

We all stared at her in disbelief. "Well," I said finally, "how about we worry about ourselves now and the abalone later? If we're still around."

She nodded and brushed her eyes with the back of her hand. "What's Patrick doing?"

We all looked over. Patrick and Victor appeared to be arguing about something. Finally, Victor shrugged and stepped back, and Patrick took his place on the bow. "Patrick's going to try to board us," Olivia said. "I wonder why?"

"Jibe again," I said wearily. "Let's do it."

We jibed again, and again, and again. I lost count of how many times we'd jibed. We were working like a team that had been together for years, each of us doing our part. Still, I didn't know how long we could keep this up. My shoulders were aching, and the palms of my hands were raw and blistered from hauling on the sheets. And we were going to run out of sea room—*Salty Mist* was pushing us to one side of the channel. A few more turns and we'd run into shallower water and *Jeopardy* would go aground.

Then we wouldn't be able to get away.

Salty Mist suddenly veered closer, and there was an awful crash. *Jeopardy* shuddered as the powerboat's hull collided with its own. Joey yelled something, and there was a deafening explosion as he set off another flare. When the smoke cleared, my ears were ringing so loudly I couldn't hear a thing. *Salty Mist* had swerved away again, and Keith was leaning over the side, checking for damage.

Olivia pointed to our bow and yelled something I couldn't make out.

Then I saw Patrick, clinging to the lifelines with one arm, his body hanging over the side of *Jeopardy*'s hull.

chapter twenty-one

We all stood frozen for a minute.

"What should we do?" Olivia whispered.

Stamp on his fingers, I was thinking, but then Patrick let go and dropped into the water.

"Jeez. That was close." Blair shook his head.

"Patrick wouldn't have hurt us," Olivia said.

I looked at her. "Sometimes, Olivia, I think you're completely nuts. He was quite content to let Victor and Keith kill us, remember?"

She nodded impatiently. "Oh, I know, I know. But he wouldn't do it himself."

A burst of static was followed by a voice over the radio: "*Jeopardy, Jeopardy.* This is the Coast Guard."

Olivia ran and picked up the microphone. "Coast Guard, this is *Jeopardy.*"

I was watching *Salty Mist.* It was hanging back, a couple of boat lengths behind us. "What are they doing?" I wondered aloud.

"Picking up Patrick, I guess. Here, Spacey, take the helm." Blair grabbed the binoculars and peered through them. "Huh."

"What?" I held the wheel with one hand and turned to see what he was looking at.

"Victor and Keith are both up top, on the fly bridge. It looks like...well, they're just standing there. Not talking or doing anything."

Salty Mist suddenly turned away from us and, quickly picking up speed, began heading back up the channel, away from Port Hardy.

"That's weird," I said slowly.

Olivia put down the microphone. "The RCMP boat is close; they say they're in the area. They're just looking for us." She turned to Joey. "Send another flare up."

Joey looked sheepish. "I don't think we have anymore. Sorry."

I shrugged. "Looks like *Salty Mist* is leaving anyway. Olivia, I think they must have been listening to the VHF. Were you on channel sixteen?"

She nodded. "Yeah. I guess they decided not to wait around for the cops."

We all started high-fiving each other. Then I realized something: They'd left Patrick behind.

Olivia and I both said it at the same time: "Patrick's still in the water." Slowly, we all turned and stared back the way we'd come. I couldn't see him.

"We have to go back," I said.

Olivia nodded, but Joey looked at me like I was nuts. "You can't be serious," he protested. "Can't he just swim until the cops get here?"

"Spacey's right," Blair said reluctantly. "What if he drowned? It'd be our fault."

Joey snorted. "Hardly." He looked at Olivia, and seeing her nod agreement with

Blair, he sighed. "Okay, okay. We'll go back for him."

I looked at the compass. "We've been heading northeast on a course of forty-five degrees," I said. "So if we want to head back the way we came, that'd be...southwest... um..."

"Two-hundred-twenty-five degrees," Olivia said.

I nodded. "Right. Maybe if two of us go up to the bow and watch for him?"

Olivia and Blair nodded. "We'll do that," Blair said.

Joey and I tacked quickly. I tightened the main sheet, and Joey hauled the jib in, using a winch handle for the last few turns to bring the sail taut. *Jeopardy* heeled over slightly and picked up speed. It was a great boat, I thought. Even with its rigging damaged, it had done everything we'd asked of it. Patrick didn't deserve it.

I squinted at the blue water. It wasn't rough, but even these small waves were enough to hide a person's head. We hadn't taken note of our mileage when Patrick had gone overboard, and I wasn't sure how much time had passed. "Do you think we've gone too far?" I asked Joey.

"Dunno. Maybe."

We sailed on for a few more minutes. Blair turned and yelled from the bow, "We must have missed him! Let's sail back and try again!"

We were about to tack when we heard Olivia shout, "There he is! There he is!"

I followed her pointing finger but still couldn't see him. "To port a little," she said. "Right there. At least, I think that's him."

Something dark bobbed in the water, a few hundred feet away. It could've been a seal, for all I could tell, or even a half-submerged log, but I turned the wheel to port slightly and let the sails out. "You think that's him?" I asked Joey.

He shook his head. "Dunno." Then he grinned. "If it is, you'd better not run him over."

"Don't tempt me," I said. I was nervous though. Getting close enough to rescue him, while avoiding actually hitting him, wasn't going to be easy. This time there was no bright orange flag that I could use to guide the boat. I'd have to rely on Olivia and Blair, up on the bow, to help me get the boat into the right position. "Joey, get the life ring ready to toss over," I told him.

Joey nodded and untied the ring from the stern rail. "Ready."

"It's him," Blair yelled. "A little more to port."

Then I could see him. He looked frantic, like he was struggling to stay afloat, and he was screaming. I turned *Jeopardy* toward him, holding my breath. "You sure I'm not going to be too close?" I shouted.

"Keep going," Blair said. "You're fine."

I didn't think I was fine. It felt just like the time I thought I ran over Joey. Too close, too close. I hesitated, wondering whether I should listen to my own instincts or trust the others.

Can't count on anyone but yourself. That was what my dad always said. But I wasn't so sure about that anymore. I gripped the wheel harder and held my course.

"Slow down," Blair shouted. "Ease the sheets."

I let out the sails, spilling the wind from them. *Jeopardy* flattened out, no longer heeling over to one side, and our speed started to drop. I turned into the wind, slowing us even more.

Olivia leaned over the side of the boat. "Patrick! Are you okay?"

"Here," Joey yelled. "Grab this." He tossed the life ring overboard. Up at the bow, Blair threw a coiled heaving line into the water.

I stood on the cockpit bench, trying to spot Patrick. I heard him before I saw him. He was swearing a blue streak and choking and spluttering in the water. We drifted past him, our momentum still carrying us forward.

Patrick splashed around, trying to swim to the life ring. "Don't leave me!"

"Give me one good reason why we shouldn't," I said, glaring at him.

"Please. I think my leg's broken."

Cry me a river, I thought. "Grab the life ring and the heaving line," I yelled as we drifted farther away. "We'll pull you in."

He started to say something but got a mouthful of salt water and started choking again.

"Shut up and swim," I shouted.

Finally he grabbed the life ring and hung on while we pulled on the rope until he was alongside *Jeopardy*.

"You know," I told him, "I want my money back. Every last penny." I heard sirens wailing and looked up just as Olivia shouted that she could see the police boat.

An aluminum-hulled boat with a forward cabin and covered cockpit was flying over the water toward us, its blue lights flashing.

On the open back deck, a fair-haired woman in a police uniform stood up and called out to us. "*Jeopardy?*"

"Yes," Olivia shouted back. "That's us."

The boat maneuvered alongside, and the sirens cut off abruptly, leaving a sudden ringing silence in their wake. "RCMP. I'm Constable Grey. Where's the boat that was chasing you?"

"They took off when they heard on the radio that you were close." Olivia pointed.

"That way. Back toward Bull Harbour."

The woman nodded. "All right. We're going to come aboard and get some more information from you."

"You're not going after them?" I asked, disappointed.

"We'll need statements from all of you first."

An older man with a mustache switched off the engine and stood up. "Constable Hilliard," he said. He passed me a line, and I tied it to a cleat, holding their boat to ours. Joey held out his hands to help Constable Hilliard aboard, followed by Constable Grey.

"Umm, who's this?" Hilliard asked, peering over the side of the boat. Patrick had suddenly become quiet when the police arrived, and Hilliard had just spotted him hanging on to his life ring a few feet away.

"He's one of them," Joey said darkly.

I tried to explain. "He owns this sailboat. He is—well, he was—our sailing instructor. But it turned out he was part of the whole abalone poaching ring, and he was on their boat. But he fell overboard and they left him, and..."

Hilliard held up one hand. "Whoa. How about we just get him on board for now? I'll need to get statements from all of you, but let's take it one step at a time."

I nodded. I suddenly felt exhausted. "We've been up all night," I said. "Sorry."

"Officer, I wouldn't have hurt these kids. I mean it." Patrick looked at me pleadingly. "Tell him, Simon. You know I wouldn't have hurt you. I tried to help you guys get away."

I shrugged. "You can tell him yourself." Part of me wanted to believe him. I'd liked him, looked up to him even. Maybe he tried to do the right thing, but I wasn't convinced. Last night, it had sure seemed like he'd been willing to let Victor and Keith get rid of us. Standing by while we were killed might not be quite as bad as killing us himself, but from where I was standing the end result looked pretty much the same.

chapter twenty-two

We managed to get Patrick onboard, but he was obviously hurting. His left leg was broken and maybe some ribs too. The RCMP called the Coast Guard, who sent a boat to pick him up and take him ashore.

"We'll send an officer to take your statement at the hospital," Constable Grey told him. Patrick just stared at her and didn't say a word.

I didn't care how much his leg hurt: I made him write four checks before he left, one for each of us. Blair and Joey laughed at me, but I didn't care. They hadn't pumped gas and waited tables to earn that money. I figured a full refund was the least he could give us. Patrick didn't argue. He pulled a damp checkbook out of a locker and signed four checks.

"Simon...sail my boat back to the marina," he said as he handed them to me. It sounded more like a plea than an order.

I met his eyes, and he looked away. I had a lump in my throat for some reason. "I will," I said. "We all will."

The two officers said that they would just get brief statements from the rest of us now, and that they'd take full statements back at the police station in Port Hardy. Their idea of brief wasn't much like mine, and it seemed to take forever. They spoke to us one at a time, taking all kinds of notes and asking a million questions.

After my turn was over, I sat in the cockpit, stared out at the sky, feeling depressed. It was all over, and it had all been for nothing. They were letting Victor and Keith get away.

I was going to have to go home and back to work and school. I hadn't got my yachting association qualification, and I was going to have to say goodbye to Joey, Blair and Olivia.

I never thought I'd feel this way, but I didn't really want to say goodbye to any of them. We were a team now, the four of us. And Olivia...well, I especially didn't want to say goodbye to Olivia.

Just then, she joined me in the cockpit. "What's with the gloomy face?" she whispered.

I shrugged, not wanting her to know too much of what I'd been thinking. "I just wish they'd go after *Salty Mist*. If the cops don't hurry, they'll never find them."

A slow smile spread across her face. "Sure they will," she said, and her grin stretched even wider. "We took all their extra fuel and their tank was almost empty, remember? All that chasing around in circles after us..." She laughed. "They won't get far. They'll be floating in the channel just waiting for the cops to come pick them up."

A huge weight lifted off my chest. I'd forgotten about their tank being so low. I put one arm around her and gave her a quick sideways hug. "Olivia, you...you're all right."

"You're not too bad yourself," she said.

Finally all our statements had been taken. "Can you get this boat back to Port Hardy on your own?" Constable Grey asked. "We need to catch up with the *Salty Mist*. And neither of us knows how to sail."

I shrugged. "Patrick asked us to take the boat back. And it shouldn't be a problem, now that no one's trying to kill us," I said. "We'll be fine. We know what we're doing."

For the first time, the two cops grinned. They got back into the RCMP boat and gave us a quick wave. "Remember, you need to go down to the police station," Constable Hilliard reminded us. He laughed. "And if you see anything suspicious between here and there, do me a favor and just keep sailing."

And then they were gone, and it was just the four of us again. We raised the sails and *Jeopardy* flew across the shining water, heading for Port Hardy. It wasn't long before we could see buildings along the shore.

"It's almost over, isn't it?" Olivia said. "I mean, this is it."

"Yup," Joey said. "I guess we're going to have to call our folks and head home." He sighed. "Man, I need a decent night's sleep."

"You've slept more than any of us," Blair said grumpily. "Anyway, I need a shower more than anything."

I laughed but I felt sad. I couldn't imagine being back at home, trying to explain all this to my parents, and going back to my job at the gas station. I looked at Patrick's check. In a few days, I thought, this would all feel unreal, like it never happened. "I wish we could just keep sailing," I said impulsively. "Just take *Jeopardy* and head south. Mexico, maybe. Or Hawaii. Or though the Panama Canal and into the Caribbean."

Olivia gasped. "Simon! You've just given me the best idea."

"What?" I looked at her. The sun was behind her, and her wild black hair was outlined with gold. "You want to steal *Jeopardy?*"

She laughed. "Better than that. I want you to come with me to the Caribbean."

I stared at her. "You mean, to sail with you and your dad and his—"

"Child-bride. Yeah." She shrugged. "It'd be more bearable if you were there too."

"But, what would your dad say?"

"I'll just tell him you're part of the deal." She made a face. "He feels so guilty about leaving me and Mom he'll agree to anything. Besides, he's been begging me to come forever. He'll be thrilled."

"You're sure?"

"Absolutely." She winked. "Plus I might mention something about how you saved my life. That won't hurt."

My cheeks were hot. "I didn't."

"Sure you did." She brushed my protests aside. "Will your parents let you come?"

I thought about it. Dad wasn't keen on sailing, but to be fair, he never stood in my way if I really wanted something. And Mom? She'd go on about how she'd miss me, but she'd be thrilled for me too. School had never been my thing, so no one would be surprised that I wasn't heading straight to college in the fall. And my folks knew I wanted to work with boats in one way or another. Of course, I'd need a plane ticket...I stuck my hands in my pockets and my fingers brushed the edge of Patrick's check. I felt a grin as wide as the ocean spreading across my face. "Yeah," I said. "They'll be cool with it."

Olivia didn't say anything. She just nodded, like everything was settled.

I looked out at the sun sparkling like tiny diamonds on the water. Maybe, I thought, delivery skippers didn't always have to sail alone.

A few years ago, Robin Stevenson bought a thirty-foot sailboat called *Tara*, fixed it up and left Lake Ontario with a plan to sail to the Bahamas. Despite knowing very little about sailing, she arrived safely in the islands a few months later. aboard her sailboat and is , British Columbia. Robin al books for children and

ut Robin and her books is : www.robinstevenson.com.

orca sports

Visit www.orcabook.com for more Orca titles.